Platinum Edition
Over 62 Million Napoleon Hill Books Read World-Wide!

How To Sell Your Way Through Life

By
NAPOLEON HILL

Lexington House

Publishers of Leading American Books and References Since 1965

Platinum Edition

Napoleon Hill in 1920 at age 37.

How To Sell Your Way Through Life by NAPOLEON HILL
This publication is designed to provide accurate and authoritative information in regard to the subject matter covered. It is published with the understanding that the publisher and author are not engaged in rendering legal, accounting, or other professional service. If legal advice or other professional advice, including financial, is required, the services of a competent professional person should be sought.

From a Declaration of Principle, jointly adopted by a Committee of the American Bar Association, and a Committee of Publishers.

Copyright © 1939, 1967 by The Napoleon Hill Foundation;
Revised Edition Copyright © 2005 The Napoleon Hill Foundation

First Authorized and Revised American Edition
Lexington House Books are available through most USA bookstores. They can also be ordered from the publisher at the below address. For permission request, write to the publisher, addressed "Attention Permissions Coordinator" at the address listed below.

Published by *Lexington House*®, 98 Dennis Drive, Lexington, Kentucky 40503 – USA
Publishers of Leading American Books and References Since 1965.
Visit our helpful website at www.kisslingorganization.com

Printed and bound in the United States of America. Printed on acid-free and recycled paper that is composed of 50% recovered fiber, including 10% post-consumer waste.
Book design by Debbie Moore.
Copy editing directed by Jan Cooper, Ph.D.
Project coordinated by Deborah Haggard Potts.

The stylized nomenclature reading *Lexington House*® is composed of a modified version of Sheer-Grace typeface and is depicted with a classic Greek or Roman building structure enclosed in a semi-circle extending from the first letter of the first word. This is a registered trademark of *Lexington House*®.

British Library Cataloguing in Publication Data available.
American Library of Congress Cataloging in Publication Data available.

Library of Congress Cataloging-in-Publication Data
Hill, Napoleon
How To Sell Your Way Through Life
(First Authorized, Revised and Expanded USA Edition)
p.cm.
ISBN 0-910882-11-8 (non-alk. paper)
12 13 14 15 16 17 18 19 20   **Platinum Edition**

Platinum Edition

HOW TO SELL
YOUR WAY
THROUGH LIFE

Highly Proven To Help Make Millionaires!
First Authorized Revised USA Edition

By

NAPOLEON HILL

Author of the Treasured Classic ***Think And Grow Rich***

Revised, Abridged, Edited, And With An Introduction By
FORREST WALLACE CATO
And
FRED R. KISSLING

ACKNOWLEDGEMENTS

Appreciation is gratefully, and sincerely, expressed for what may be the world's greatest team of fact-checkers and proofreaders, all dedicated to insuring accuracy and compliance with the original Napoleon Hill text featured in this Platinum Edition of **How To Sell Your Way Through Life**.

Serving as Chairman of this group was Jan Cooper, Ph.D. Dr. Cooper's involved Napoleon Hill scholars included Joan Berry Ed.D.; Charlie "Tremendous" Jones, RFC; H. Aaron Meyers Jr; Bill Warder, AIFA ; John F. Post; J. Steve Blount, PRC; and William R. Lindsey, RFC.

Thanks also are due the award-winning photographer Tim Cox. Photography by Tim Cox helped Make "Napoleon Hill Country" better known around the world. Some of Tim's photos are used in this volume with his kind permission. Tim Cox also arranged for us to obtain and publish the historical coal mining photos featured in this book.

Appreciation is especially owed to Deborah Haggard Potts for her tireless assistance, and for her thorough, meticulous, and efficient coordination of this important publishing project from beginning to end.

The publishers are deeply grateful for having been granted access to the Napoleon Hill Photo Archives.

List of Archival and Current Photos

CONTENTS

INTRODUCTION
Forrest Wallace Cato, RFC, CRR, CPC
(Best-Selling Author, Award-Winning Magazine Editor,
And Multi-National Media Advocate)

You are going to ask! So up front in this Platinum Edition, even before you start to seek this information, I will immediately answer your questions. Before you finish reading Napoleon Hill's *How To Sell Your Way Through Life,* you will most likely want to know the following.

Your first question will be: "How can I contact The Napoleon Hill World Learning Center?"

Your second question may be: "How can I contact The Napoleon Hill Foundation?"

You may also have other related questions about contacts. So, here in advance, are the contact details you may need. Remember to return to this page when you realize you need this information.

1. **Judith Williamson**
   Director
   The Napoleon Hill World Learning Center
   (A non-profit education organization located at
   Purdue University Calumet.)
   2300 173rd Street
   Hammond, Indiana 46323 – USA
   Phone: 219-989-3173 or 219-989-3166
   Fax: 219-989-3174
   E-mail: nhf@calumet.purdue.edu
   Website: www.naphil.org

You may also direct inquiries to Uriel Martinez at the above address.

2. **Don M. Green**
   Executive Director
   The Napoleon Hill Foundation
   (A non-profit educational institution)
   P. O. Box 1277
   Wise, Va. 24293 – USA
   Phone: 276-328-6700
   Fax: 276-328-8752
   E-mail: napoleonhill@uvawise.edu

THE DIRECTOR OF
THE NAPOLEON HILL WORLD LEARNING CENTER

Judith A. Williamson is the acclaimed Director of the Napoleon Hill World Learning Center at Purdue University Calumet, Hammond, Indiana. Dr. Williamson is responsible for directing and managing the operations, including course offerings for credit and continuing education, creation and maintenance of new and existing materials, presentation of seminars locally, nationally, and internationally, and program cost recovery. She is known as "The professional administrator/educator with a heart!"

Dr. Williamson has served in increasingly responsible positions of Development for over 20 years. She is skilled in Development, School Administration, Program Planning, Staff Evaluation and Instruction. She is an award-winning Director of Development, Principal, and University Instructor. Her platform talents include speaking on Dr. Hill's Science of Success, annual giving, grants management, planned giving, program development, grants maintenance and fundraising.

Major areas of her involvement include, but are not limited to,

Certification of instructors for the Hill Foundation

K-12 School Curriculum

Creation of new materials

Seminar Presentation Management

Maintenance of Napoleon Hill World Learning Center

Order fulfillment via mail and website

International relations

Training of clients licensed with the Napoleon Hill Foundation

Cost recovery and organizational management

A life-long student of Napoleon Hill, Judith Williamson also maintains her own library of self-help, personal motivation, and inspirational guidance references. She has worked in close liaison with many educators, trainers, and conference or convention planners.

According to Dr. Williamson, "One of the greatest satisfactions of my work is when people come back stage, or approach me in the lobby, or write, and tell me how the works of Dr. Napoleon Hill have helped them today. For example, during a recent speaking engagement in London, two British audience members told me about how they had each achieved major personal goals in 2002 by following the lessons of Dr. Hill."

THE NAPOLEON HILL FOUNDATION
EXECUTIVE DIRECTOR

Don M. Green, a well-known and highly respected former bank president, now retired, continues as an active senior executive and civic leader. He is also a leading tourism booster for Wise County, Virginia, also known as Napoleon Hill Country. Mr. Green is a life-long fan of Appalachian mountain-style bluegrass music. His neighbor and long-time friend is Dr. Ralph Stanley the world-acclaimed musician who's 55-plus (years-long) singing career has ignited internationally since Stanley performed numbers like *Oh Death* a solo, and *Angel Band* with his Clinch Mountain Boys, in the soundtrack for the movie, *O Brother, Where Art Thou?* Both Green and Stanley call it "American music." Stanley explains, "It's just down to earth and deep in the roots, natural." Both men are known for their quiet, low-key, unassuming demeanor, and rich Southern charm that immediately enables others to be at ease in their presence. They win friends effortlessly.

Mr. Green is also currently "highly booked" — for his platform talents. Mr. Green modestly explains, "This is largely because of the huge renewed interest in the life and works of Dr. Napoleon Hill." As possibly America's leading authority on Napoleon Hill, Mr. Green now receives ongoing request to speak on the life and works of Dr. Hill. As time permits, Mr. Green considers each related speaking request, after a formal inquiry, or request, has been submitted in writing.

Mr. Green directs and administers the trademarks, copyrights, publications, licensing, photos, and agreement renewals, both nationally and internationally, as the chief official representative for the Napoleon Hill Foundation. He also directs, or manages, all related functions. Mr. Green coordinates all ongoing legal activities.

Weekly Mr. Green fields the endless requests from motivational speakers, sales trainers, consultants, and others, who seek "to ride on Napoleon Hill's coat-tails" by attempting to have their names associated with Dr. Hill's in some type of video, CD, book, music, recording, other publication, or product. Mr. Green is frequently available to the media, and others, for interviews, and to speak via telephone regarding Napoleon Hill's entire history and background, or on Dr. Hill's career, his "body" of works, or on Dr. Hill's upbringing in historic Wise County, Virginia.

AN OVERVIEW TODAY

The Napoleon Hill World Learning Center is the educational component of the Napoleon Hill Foundation. Located just minutes from downtown Chicago, in Hammond, Indiana, the Napoleon Hill World Learning Center provides educational opportunities for students of Napoleon Hill's Philosophy of Success. Established with a one million dollar grant from the Napoleon Hill Foundation, the Learning Center's mission parallels the mission of the Foundation.

**Napoleon Hill Foundation
Mission Statement**

*A non-profit, charitable, educational institution,
dedicated to making the world a better place in which
to work and live, and helping empower and enable
people to reach their realistic and worthy goals.*

As an educational center, their goal is to disseminate Napoleon Hill's works to each individual and all open and interested audiences. Currently their focus includes university students as well as the correctional population nationwide. However, it is also their immediate goal to impact K-12 instruction with Hill's 17 Principles of Success. Both an elementary and a secondary program are being refined for the purpose of use in both public and private school settings.

As the international hub of the Napoleon Hill Foundation, the Napoleon Hill World Learning Center (NHWLC) aims to increase personal success through life-long education. Located at The Center, the NHWLC houses W. Clement Stone's personal library, Hill's classic works, and Dr. Hill's archival materials, and other motivational, inspirational, self-help, sales training, and entrepreneurial literature. Classes on Dr. Hill's success philosophy are available on the graduate, undergraduate, and non-credit levels.

Forrest Wallace Cato

About Forrest Wallace Cato

Forrest Wallace Cato, RFC, CRR, CPC, is a reviewer, essayist, scholar, and critic. According to the syndicated business columnist, Mickey M. Greenfield, JD, Ph.D., "Cato is a national award-winning financial magazine editor. Plus, for over twenty-five-years Cato has also served as a Media Advocate for leading financial professionals in the USA, England, Singapore, Malaysia, Thailand, and Hong Kong." Dr. Greenfield explains, "A Media Advocate helps your market recognize your significance or the significance of your product or service."

Cato is former Editor of *Financial Planning* Magazine and *Trusts & Estates: The Journal of Wealth Management*. Presently Cato edits *Financial Services Advisor* Magazine, an 82 year old journal read by the 20% of financial advisors who sell, each year, approximately 80% of the financial products and services sold in America.

He is also Editor-in-Chief of *The Inspirator International*, the largest circulation English language magazine providing sales training and inspirational motivation, in all of the Pacific-Rim countries.

Cato's writings have been published in the USA, England, Canada, Japan, South Korea, Taiwan, Hong Kong, Thailand, South Africa, Philippines, Malaysia, India, Singapore, Indonesia, parts of China, plus the United Kingdom (England, Ireland, Scotland, and Wales) Australia, and New Zealand.

Annually he presents The Cato Award for outstanding accomplishments in financial writing during the yearly convention of the International Association of Registered Financial Consultants.

PREFACE

Fred R. Kissling, Jr., CLU, MSPA, AEP, RFC
*(America's Leading Independent Publisher of Sales References
For Insurance Agents And Financial Planners)*

The spirit in which Napoleon Hill approached, created, and finished writing *How To Sell Your Way Through Life* is explained in the following frontice piece by Dr. Hill. This is reprinted here word-by-word:

> LIFE, you can't subdue me, because I refuse to take your discipline seriously.
>
> When you try to hurt me, I laugh, and laughter knows no pain.
>
> I appropriate your joys whenever I find them. Your sorrows neither discourage nor frighten me, for there is laughter in my soul.
>
> When I get what I want, I am glad, but temporary defeat does not make me sad. I simply set music to the words of defeat and turn defeat into a song about laughter.
>
> Your tears are not for me. I like laughter much better, and because I like laughter. I use laughter as a substitute for grief and sorrow and pain and disappointment.
>
> Life, you are a fickle trickster, don't deny it!
>
> You slipped the emotion of love into my heart so you might use it as a thorn with which to prick my soul, but I have learned to dodge your trap. . .with laughter.
>
> You try to lure me with the desire for gold, but I have outwitted you by following the trail which leads to knowledge, instead.

You induce me to build beautiful friendships; then convert my friends into enemies, so you may harden my heart, but I sidestep your fickleness by laughing off your attempt and selecting new friends in my own way.

You cause men to cheat me in trade, so I will become hard and irritable, but I win again because I possess only one precious asset, and this is something no man can steal. . .IT IS THE POWER TO THINK MY OWN THOUGHTS AND BE MYSELF, plus the capacity to laugh at you for your efforts.

You threaten me with Death, but to me Death is nothing worse than a long, peaceful sleep, and sleep is the sweetest of human experiences. . .except laughter.

You build the fire of Hope in my breast, then sprinkle water on the flames, but I go you one better by rekindling the fire on my own account. . .and laugh at you once more!

You plant vicious enemies in my path who try to assault my reputation and destroy my self-reliance, but you fail again because I turn their efforts into publicity which brings me to the attention of new friends whom I would never know otherwise.

For a quarter of a century, you hurdle-jumped me over every conceivable form of failure, but I coined the knowledge gained from these failures into a philosophy of Success which now renders useful service and brings countless thousands of others the joy of laughter; and these newly made friends willingly pay me compound interest for every second of failure you have imposed upon me.

You bore me into this world in poverty, but this has proved to be a blessing in disguise because poverty has taught me patience and industry and imagination and temperance and humility and a hundred other useful traits which the idle will never know.

Life, you are licked as far as I am concerned, because you have nothing with which to lure me away from laughter and you are powerless to scare me.

WORLDWIDE, NAPOLEON HILL HAS SOLD
OVER 62 MILLION BOOKS!

Of all the successful Napoleon Hill titles, *How To Sell Your Way Through Life* remains one of his most universally popular books. This volume is the perennial favorite of professionals who must sell their service and also the favorite of sales men and women the world over. Insurance sales legend Mehdi Fakharzadeh says, "Successful sales professionals across our globe owe a huge debt to Napoleon Hill!" It is often reported that this work is "...The most effective and the most successful sales training and achievement guide of all time!" No other sales reference is more used in the fields of insurance, financial planning, real estate, or any other "big ticket" sales.

Here is more of what Napoleon Hill had to say about *How to Sell Your Way Through Life* reproduced here in this special Platinum Edition:

This book was not written for the purpose of expressing heroism or brilliancy. Its sole purpose is to convey practical information that is known to be sound because it was obtained from the life experiences of hundreds of successful sales people who began at scratch and made for themselves enviable positions in the world. For this reason the book should be the handbook of every person who has just finished school and is ready to sell himself through life successfully. If I could place a copy of the book in the hands of all sales people and members of every family having children of high school age, and every person graduating from college, I would feel I made a definite contribution to the successful lives of hundreds of thousands of young people who are today striving for their paths that lead to self-determination.

ABOUT FRED R. KISSLING, JR.

Fred R. Kissling, Jr., CLU, MSPA, AEP, RFC, is the CEO of The Kissling Organization, headquartered in Lexington, Kentucky. This firm is America's largest independent financial publishing corporation. The organization he directs publishes *Financial Services Advisor*® magazine, a famous 83-year-old journal for financial advisors. This respected trade publication is read by the approximate 20% of financial professionals who, each year, sell about 80% of America's financial products and services.

The Kissling Organization also publishes the influential *Probe*® newsletter which is avidly read by senior financial executives and "financial leaders" throughout America's financial industries.

Kissling also serves as publisher of *Financial & Estate Planner's Quarterly.*®

The Kentucky citizen is also publisher of *Leaders*® magazine, which serves the life insurance industry. *Leaders*® was founded in 1938.

He produces *Fraternal Monitor*®, the only magazine serving the USA's fraternal insurance industry. *Fraternal Monitor*® is 114 years old.

Kissling's organization also publishes *The Disability & Long Term Care Advisory*®, read by practitioners of various related financial disciplines who are members of the estate planning team.

The Kissling Organization also owns *Lexington House*®. Since 1965, *Lexington House*® has served as a leading American publisher of references and books covering sales, personal and professional success, plus insurance and financial planning.

Kissling is the only financial publisher in America who has served as President of the American Society of Pension Actuaries, the Association for Advanced Life Underwriting, and the National Association of Estate Planning Councils.

Kissling is a life member of the Million Dollar Round Table. He has been a member for 50 years. The MDRT is an organization of top insurance sales achievers.

Kissling is the author of several well-known books and is a highly-booked speaker both nationally and internationally. He frequently writes on improving sales and client relations. His articles have been published in Japan, Hong Kong, Taiwan, Malaysia, Singapore, Thailand and parts of China.

A Kentucky resident, he is the owner of racehorses and is a breeder of thoroughbreds. His horses have participated in major races across the US and his stables contain the champion Spanish Glitter.

Kissling has served three terms as President of the Lexington, Kentucky Chapter of the Society of Financial Services Professionals (CLU and ChFC). He has served as general chairman of the United Way of the Bluegrass and chairman of the Salvation Army.

Kissling is listed in *Who's Who in the World*, *Who's Who in America*, and *Who's Who in the South and Southwest*.

AUTHOR'S PREFACE
Napoleon Hill
*(World's Most Successful Sales And Success Trainer, and Founder of
The World's Self-Help And Personal Achievement Movement)*

Many years ago, a young man dropped from a moving freight train in East Orange, New Jersey and hurriedly made his way to the laboratory of Thomas A. Edison. When asked to state his business, before being permitted to see Mr. Edison, the young man boldly replied, "I am going to become his partner!"

His boldness got him past the secretary. An hour later he was at work, scrubbing floors in the Edison plant. Five years later, he was a partner of the great Edison. The man's name is Edwin C. Barnes, once known throughout the United States as the distributor of the Ediphone dictating machine. His home was in Florida, not very far from my own home. I have known him for a quarter of a century; have known him through the relationship of close personal friendship that gives me the privilege of saying that he sold himself to Edison through the psychology of selling described in this book.

Edwin Barnes accumulated a fortune far greater than he needed, and he owed every cent of it to the hour he spent in private conversation with Edison. During that hour, he sold himself so thoroughly that it gave him his opportunity to go into partnership with one of the greatest men this country ever produced. Roughly speaking, that hour of selling was worth in actual cash the millions of dollars Edwin Barnes afterwards accumulated.

My first job was that of secretary to General Rufus A. Ayers, for whom I went to work while I was still in my teens. Long before I was 20, I became the General Manager of one of General Ayers' coal mines. The jump from secretary to General Manager was made in less than one hour, during which I sold myself into the better position by voluntarily rendering confidential service for which I neither expected nor asked pay. That sale changed the entire trend of my life and led directly to my alliance with Andrew Carnegie, with its far-flung effects on myself and thousands of others.

If you asked me to tell you why this book may be of benefit to you, and demanded I give you proof that I am an authority on *How to Sell Your Way Through Life*, I would be compelled to pull aside the curtains which hide from view my private life and give you the information in these frank, but truthful words:

Years ago I began, at the request of, and in collaboration with, Andrew Carnegie, to organize all the causes of success and failure into a philosophy of individual achievement. During those 30 years of research, it became necessary for me to contact, interview, and gain the cooperation of the most successful men in the country, including Henry Ford, Thomas A. Edison, John Wanamaker, Luther Burbank, Woodrow Wilson, and others of their type from whose rich experiences I organized the first practical philosophy of individual achievement, under the title of *Law of Success*.

The best evidence the philosophy is sound and practical may be found in the use I have made of it in selling my way through life. The blessings this philosophy has given me are many, the greatest of them being the fact I can truthfully say I have sold my way through life so successfully that I have everything I need or can use for the attainment of happiness, including of course, absolute freedom from all manner of worry over money.

I am married to the woman of my choice, with whom I have found harmony and understanding sufficient to give me continuous peace of mind and inspiration to hitch my wagon to higher stars than any I had aspired to reach before I found her.

Having converted my philosophy into the privilege of living my own life, in my own chosen way, in any part of the world I desire, Mrs. Hill and I have established a permanent home in Mount Dora, Florida, where we have an abundance of sunshine, in a Castle surrounded by trees and fresh air, far enough removed from the rest of the world to give us privacy, close enough to keep us attuned to the hearts and minds of our neighbors.

From one to three hours out of every twenty-four we devote to our private Master Mind conference at which we analyze our plans and prepare some form of service for the benefit of others who have been less successful than we in selling their way through life.

We have no fears of any nature whatsoever. We have no worries. We have no feeling of suspense over the past, the present or the future. We have good health. We have open minds toward all things and all people, and we make it our business to learn something of interest or value from every person we contact.

The philosophy with which Mrs. Hill and I have sold our way into happiness is fully and frankly described in this book. The spirit of our philosophy may be found in the challenge to life which I wrote years ago, the day after the depression had shut off my income and destroyed my entire fortune.

The rhythm of our Florida home is both positive and contagious because it has been established by a blending of the minds of two people who are doing exactly what they wish to do and through their work have found supreme happiness. This environmental rhythm is so definite it affects everyone who contacts it, including all the members of our household, our secretaries, our adopted children, and all who visit us. It is so noticeable that it is the first thing our visitors observe when they enter our home, and always they speak of the inspiring effect it has upon them.

This same rhythm of opulence and peace of mind has been written into the lines of this book, every word of which was carefully examined, weighed and evaluated by both Mrs. Hill and myself before the manuscript was given to the publisher. We would be greatly surprised if any reader of the book failed to pick up the influence of this rhythm as he or she reads.

Napoleon Hill

ABOUT NAPOLEON HILL

Napoleon Hill, Ph.D., was born in 1883 in a one-room cabin on the Pound River in Wise County, Virginia. He began his career working in a coal mine. He became a mine manager while still a teenager. His writing career started at age 13 as a "mountain reporter" for small town newspapers. He went on to become America's, then the world's most beloved motivational author.

Hill passed away in November 1970 after a long and successful career writing, teaching, and lecturing about the principles of success. His work stands as a monument to individual achievement and is the cornerstone of modern motivation. More people have achieved success, using his methods, than from any other source.

His book, *Think and Grow Rich,* is the all time bestseller in the field. Hill established his Foundation as a nonprofit educational institution whose mission is to perpetuate his philosophy of leadership, self-motivation, and individual achievement.

His books, audio cassettes, videotapes, and other self-help products are made available to you as a service of the Napoleon Hill World Learning Center so that you may build your own library of personal achievement materials, and to assist you in acquiring the financial wealth and the true riches of life.

PART ONE

CHARACTER IS ACCURATELY REFLECTED IN ONE'S MENTAL ATTITUDE

"Without a strong foundation built on positive character traits, success will not long endure. It is virtually impossible to fake good character. Phonies are quickly spotted because they haven't the substance and determination to maintain the charade.

Developing good character begins with a positive attitude. Your desire to be a good, decent, honest, considerate person must first take place in your mind. When you make the decision to become a person of character, you will also find that you are much more willing to do the right thing simply because it is the right thing to do."

– Napoleon Hill

CHAPTER 1
Definition of Salesmanship

A Master Salesman is an artist who can paint word pictures in the hearts of men as skillfully as Rembrandt could blend colors on a canvas. He is an artist who can play a symphony on the human emotions as effectively as Paderewski can manipulate the keys of a piano.

A Master Salesman is a strategist at mind manipulation. He can marshal the *thoughts* of men as ably as Foch directed the allied armies during the World War.

A Master Salesman is a philosopher who can interpret *causes* by their *effects* and *effects* by their *causes*.

A Master Salesman is a character analyst. He knows men as Einstein knew higher mathematics.

A Master Salesman is a mind reader. He knows what thoughts are in men's minds by the expressions on their faces, by the words they utter, by their silence, and by the "feeling" which he experiences from within, while in their presence.

The Master Salesman is a "Fortune Teller." He can predict the future by observing what has happened in the past.

The Master Salesman is a *master of others BECAUSE HE IS MASTER OF HIMSELF!*

That attributes of mastery in selling will be described in this book. Also, the means by which these qualities may be acquired. The purpose of the book is to enable the reader to transform mediocrity into mastery in *the art of persuasion.*

Life is a series of ever-changing and shifting circumstances and experiences. No two experiences are alike. No two people are alike. Day after day we experience life's kaleidoscope of changes. This makes it necessary for us to adapt ourselves to people who think and act in ways different from our own. Our success depends, very largely, upon how well we negotiate our way through these daily contacts with other people *without friction* or opposition.

This sort of negotiation calls for an understanding of the art of salesmanship. We are all salesmen, regardless of our calling. But not all of us are *master salesmen!*

The politician must sell his way into office. If he remains in office, he must keep himself sold to his constituency.

The salaried person must sell himself into a job. Salesmanship must be used to keep the position after it has been obtained.

If a man seeks a loan at a bank, he must sell the banker on making the loan.

The clergyman must sell his sermons, and himself as well, to his followers. If he is a poor salesman, he soon finds himself looking for another "call".

The lawyer must sell the merits of his client's case to the judge and jury even if he knows his case has but little merit.

If a man chooses to marry, he must sell himself to the woman of his choice. Albeit, the woman may, and often does, remove many of the obstacles in the path of the sale.

Everybody will agree with this statement.

The day laborer must sell himself to his employer, although the form of salesmanship required is not as difficult as that which must be employed by the man who sells himself into a job at $65,000.00 a year.

These are examples of salesmanship through which people sell intangibles. Any form of effort through which one person persuades another to cooperate is salesmanship. Most efforts at salesmanship are weak; and for this reason most people are poor salesmen.

If a man attains a high station in life, it is because he has acquired or was blessed with a natural ability as a salesman. Schooling, college degrees, intellect, brilliancy, are of no avail to the man who lacks the ability to attract the cooperative efforts of others, thus to *create opportunities for himself*. These qualities help a man to make the most of *opportunity* once he gets it. But he must first contact or create the opportunity to be worked on. Perhaps, by the law of averages *opportunity* is thrust upon one out of every hundred thousand people. The others must create *opportunity.* Moreover, salesmanship is often as necessary in the development of *opportunity* as in its creation.

"Salesmanship" in this book applies not merely to marketing commodities and services. *You can sell your personality. You must do it!* As a matter of fact, the major object in writing this book was to teach men and women how to sell their way through life successfully, using the "selling strategy" and the psychology used by the Master Salesman in selling goods and services.

Herbert Hoover was handicapped during his youth by the loss of his parents. Millions of other orphans have lived and died without having had the *opportunity* to make themselves known outside of the local communities in which they have *existed.* What distinguishing features did Mr. Hoover possess to enable him to set his sails in the direction of the White House and ride the winds of fortune to that high goal? *He discovered how to sell his way through life successfully.* This book is to teach others to do the same.

Jean Beltrand has given five definitions of salesmanship, as follows:

FIRST: Selling is the ability to make known your *faith, goods* or *propositions* to a person or persons to a point of creating a desire for a privilege, an opportunity, possession, or an interest.

SECOND: Selling is the ability of professional and public men to *render services, assistance,* and *cooperation* to a point of creating a desire on the part of the people to remunerate, recognize, and honor.

THIRD: Selling is the ability to *perform work, duties* and *services* as an employee, to a point of creating a desire on the part of an employer to remunerate, promote, and praise.

FOURTH: Selling is the ability to be *polite, kind, agreeable,* and *considerate* to a point of creating a desire upon the part of those you meet to respect, love, and honor you.

The great Thomas Edison failed ten thousand times before he made the incandescent electric light work. Do not become discouraged and "quit" if you fail once or twice before making your plans work.

FIFTH: Selling is the ability to write, design, paint, invent, create, compose, or accomplish anything to a point of creating a desire upon the part of the people to acclaim its possessors as heroes, celebrities, and great men.

These definitions are very broad. They might easily cover a great variety of all human activity. The whole of any life is one long, unbroken chain of sales endeavor.

The newly born babe is a salesman! When it wants food, it *yells* for it and *gets* it! When it is in pain, it *yells* for attention and *gets* that too.

Women are the greatest salespeople on earth. They are superior to men because they are more subtle, more dramatic, and use greater finesse. Men often believe they are selling themselves to women in proposals of marriage. Generally, however, it is the woman who does the selling. *She does it by making herself charming, attractive and alluring.*

While Mr. Beltrand's definitions are comprehensive, I would add to his list one more, namely—

"Selling is the art of planting in the mind of another a *motive* which will induce favorable *action*."

The importance of this definition will be apparent throughout the book.

The Master Salesman becomes a master because of his or her ability to induce other people to act upon motives without resistance or friction.

There is but little comparison with Master Salesmen because there are so few of them!

Master Salesmen *know what they want*. They know how to *plan* the acquiring of what they want. Moreover, they have the *initiative* to put into *action* such a *plan*.

There are two forms of sales endeavor. One: when the salesman is negotiating with but one person. Two: when the salesman is negotiating with a group of people. The latter is commonly known as group selling, or public speaking.

The Master Salesman's education is not complete unless he has the ability to persuade groups of people as well as influence individuals. The ability to speak to groups with that force which carries conviction is a priceless asset. It has given more than one man his *big opportunity*. This ability must be self-acquired. It is an art, which can be acquired only through study, effort, and experience.

Here are some specific instances.

William Jennings Bryan lifted himself from obscurity to a position of national prominence through his famous "Cross of Gold" speech, during a Democratic Convention.

Patrick Henry immortalized himself though his famous "Give me liberty or give me death" speech in the days of the American Revolution. But for that speech, his name might never have known its heritage.

Robert Ingersoll changed the trend of theology by his eloquent art in forceful group salesmanship.

The Master Salesman has the ability to influence people through the printed page as well as by the spoken word.

Elbert Hubbard accumulated a modest fortune and indelibly impressed his name upon the minds of men through the selling power of his pen.

Perhaps Thomas Paine, through the power of his pen, did more than other one person to inspire the American Revolution.

Benjamin Franklin immortalized himself and left his imprint for good upon civilization by the forceful simplicity and quaintness of his written salesmanship.

Abraham Lincoln immortalized himself through a single speech, his Gettysburg Address—simple in theme, pure in composition, moving in thought.

The spirit of Jesus Christ goes marching on influencing hundreds of millions of people two thousand years after his death because he was a Master Salesman. He built his sales presentation around a *motive* universally acceptable.

Caesar, Alexander, Napoleon, the ex-kaiser Wilhelm of Germany, and hundreds of others of their type were also Master Salesmen. But *they built their sales presentations around motives which were destructive of the best impulses in civilization.* They sold and delivered wars—wars for which the people paid in blood and tears and suffering.

Enduring success in selling is always predicated upon *sound motive!* Remember this, you who aspire to mastery in selling. Sell neither stones nor serpents nor swords!

The world now faces the greatest opportunity for Master Salesmanship in history. The Business Depression left wounds in millions of hearts, which must be healed. Only *master salesmanship* can do it. New leaders and a new brand leadership are needed throughout the world in almost every line of human endeavor. This is the great reconstruction period. It is rich with opportunity for Master Salesmen who have the *imagination* to build their sales efforts around *motives* which are beneficial to the general public, and who release their full *energies* through work.

Class privileges are passing! Mass privileges are in the ascendancy. Remember this, too, when selecting a *motive* as the guiding spirit of your sales efforts: The *people* must be served.

The whole of America stands at the crossroads of progress, waiting for able leadership. Millions of people have been slowed down by *fear* and *indecision.* Here is an unparalleled opportunity for men and women who are prepared to adapt themselves to the new brand of leadership, fortified by *courage*, dedicated to *service.*

High-pressure salesmanship is proven to be ineffective.

The successful leader of the future, whether in the field of selling or in other walks of life, must make the *golden rule* the basis of his leadership.

In the future the question of paramount importance will be *"How much can I give in the way of service to others,"* not, *"How much can I get away with and keep out of jail?"*

A great economic renaissance is sweeping *the entire world!*

The man who cannot see this is mentally and morally *blind.* The old order of things in business and industry has already been swept away, and a new order is rapidly taking its place. Wise beyond description is the person who sees this change and adapts himself to it harmoniously— without force!

We are approaching an era during which we will see the reincarnation of the spirit of Thomas Jefferson and Benjamin Franklin and George Washington and Abraham Lincoln in politics. And the reincarnation of the spirit of Marshall Field and John Wanamaker in the fields of industry, business, and finance.

The people have become rebellious against the oppression forced upon them by avaricious and the greedy. This spirit of resentment is not transient. It will remain until it rights a wrong. It will gain organized momentum. America will not soon again see the sad spectacle of millions of people starving to death in the midst of an overabundance of both the necessities and the luxuries of life.

We are on the Grand Concourse which leads out of the wilderness of human exploitation, and we are not going to be driven or coerced into giving up our rights to remain on this highway.

These statements of *fact* and prophecy may be helpful to those who aspire to leadership in the field of selling or in some other walk of life. Men who have *imagination* will not wait for *time* to prove their soundness. They will anticipate the changes that are to take place; and will adapt themselves to the new conditions.

The great changes occasioned by the economic upheaval which has thrown millions out of adjustment in all fields of human activity accentuates the need for discovering those fundamental principles by which one may come back into the path of ordered progress. Since all people must use some form of salesmanship to right themselves and to adjust themselves into satisfactory relations, both social and commercial, it behooves one to lend an ear to a presentation of those fundamental principles with suggestions of their practical application. This book attempts to teach principles.

The person who masters these fundamental principles of persuasion can sell his way through life successfully, surmounting obstacles, overcoming opposition, harnessing and redirecting adverse forces.

No matter who you are or how much you know, you will not succeed unless you are a salesman! You *must* sell your services. You *must* sell your knowledge. You *must* sell yourself. You *must* sell your personality.

As you approach the study of fundamentals, keep ever before you the fact that *your only limitations are creatures of your own mind.* Remember too, you can remove any limitation which you can create.

This book was written for men and women who will not permit themselves to be bound down by blind circumstances nor hedged in by psychological limitations.

* * * * *

"Ideas are the beginning points of all fortunes."
— Napoleon Hill

* * * * *

CHAPTER 2
You Need Intelligent Promotion To Succeed

I t may be true that the world will make a beaten path to your door if you make a better mouse-trap than your neighbor, even though your house may be far back in the woods, but you may as well know that the big rush toward your place of business will not begin until you have given the location and have been properly "promoted".

Jack Dempsey was an unknown prizefighter and a good one at that perhaps, but he stepped up front and became the World Championship, with a million-dollar income, only after Jack Kearns had "promoted" him into that highly desirable position. Jack Dempsey's fists and arms did the punching, but Jack Kearns' brains did the guiding of the blows so they found their way into big bank balances. The promoting job that Kearns did for Dempsey was so effective that even now, long after the championship was lost, Dempsey is able to collect big dividends for the mere use of his name.

Thomas A. Edison, with less than three months of "schooling" became "the world's greatest inventor" because he possessed that rare quality of being able to promote himself. Where he succeeded no fewer than ten thousand other inventors, many of them as capable as he, never have been heard of, and never will be.

Arthur Brisbane was a run of the mill newspaper man, no better or worse than a thousand others in his profession, until William Randolph Hearst spread his name on the front page of his newspapers; then he became America's leading columnist. I can name a hundred men who can write better stuff than anything Brisbane ever wrote, but you would not recognize one of them because they have not been properly promoted.

During the World War my attention was called to a man by the name of Arthur Nash, a Cincinnati merchant tailor, who had taken his employees into business with him and had given them a part of the profits because his business was on the rocks and he saw no other way of saving it form bankruptcy. I went to Cincinnati, interviewed Nash, and wrote the first story about him. In my story I called him "Golden Rule" Nash. The story was taken up by the newspapers and magazines of the country and he received free publicity for more than five years. When he died, a dozen years later, he was a wealthy man and his business was among the more successful of its type.

Kate Smith as all who know her will testify, is "a dear sweet girl" who sings on the radio. Kate does not have anything but a fine character and pleasing voice, but *she does have* Ted Collins, therefore she draws a weekly salary of a staggering figure, to say nothing of side incomes from moving pictures, etc.

Edgar Bergen and Charley McCarthy trooped up and down Broadway, eating now and then when the now famous pair could get an engagement, until one night when they appeared on the Rudy Vallee program. The "promotion" they received on that occasion gave them a start toward radio stardom that has made the pair among the best features of the air. Bergen was as good years ago as he was at his peak, but he was not properly promoted, so he often found himself "temporarily at leisure".

Ely Culbertson was a competent bridge player, but nothing to brag about until his wife began promoting him, and now he receives free publicity in newspapers throughout the nation. Moreover, he has made himself wealthy as a bridge "expert". He is probably no more an expert now than he was when his wife began to promote him, *but he is better paid!*

Ziegfeld picked up Will Rogers when he was an unknown gum-chewing, rope-throwing vaudeville specialist (when he could get an engagement). By proper promotion Ziegfeld catapulted Rogers into stardom almost overnight, to stay nothing of paving the way for moving picture and other moneymaking opportunities from which Rogers made millions of dollars. Before Ziegfeld promotion caught up with him,

Rogers was glad to do his stunts before clubs and on other occasions for his lunch, in cities where he was playing on the vaudeville stage. This same "promoter" took over the banjo-eyed Eddie Cantor and started him on a career that is said to now pay him $10,000 a week for merely reading lines which someone else writes! Not bad, eh? Ziegfeld also "promoted" the tall, slender Fanny Brice into the big money. Not one of these favorites would have piled up the huge fortunes the public has paid them to do their parlor tricks if it had not been for clever promotion.

When I was organizing *The Law of Success* philosophy Andrew Carnegie sent me to call on Henry Ford. "You want to watch this man Ford," said Carnegie, "for one day he is going to dominate the motor industry of America". I went to Detroit and met Ford for the first time. That was in 1908. When I first looked him over I wondered how as shrewd a judge of men Andrew Carnegie could have been so definitely mistaken in his estimation of Ford, but that was thirty years ago. Year by year I watched Ford climb to the top in his field, and back of his stupendous achievement I have observed highly organized, systematic and effective "promotion". Perhaps no man who was ever connected with the Ford promotion was of greater service to him than the late Senator Couzens, unless it is W. J. Carmeron, the present chief Ford promoter, who sees to it that the Ford interests are never neglected in the eyes of the public. Since Ford began business I have seen no less than a hundred other makers of automobiles rise and fall like mushrooms because they had not the foresight to surround themselves with promotion experts.

By "promotion experts" I do not mean advertising men. Promotion is one thing, advertising is something entirely different. Promotion, the sort to which I have reference, is the art of keeping an individual favorably sold to the public all the time.

The late Ivy Lee was one of the greatest promotion men of his time. It was he who removed the odium from the name of the elder Rockefeller and kept that name before the public in a favorable light almost continuously. Ivy Lee seldom worked through paid publicity. He preferred free space and other forms of more efficient promotion for keeping his clients properly sold to the public. While I was publishing the *Golden Rule Magazine* I wrote a brief editorial praising the work of John

All anyone really requires, as a capital on which to start a successful career, is a sound mind, a healthy body, and a genuine desire to be of as much service as possible to as many people as possible.

D. Rockefeller, Jr., in connection with his fine humanitarian work in going to Colorado to settle the famous coal strike, in 1919. Almost before the print had dried on my article I received a wire from Ivy Lee, inviting me to visit him in New York. When I met him, he got down to business without ceremonies, offering me $10,000.00 a year to join his staff and write similar editorials about other clients of his. Promotion experts earn and receive big money because they have the ability to recognize, and the good sense to appropriate the forces needed to further the interests of their clients.

During my negotiations with Ivy Lee I was astounded to learn that the world-famous Billy Sunday revivals were a well organized, Ivy Lee-guided promotion! Sunday fought the Devil up one side of the country and down the other to the tune of millions of dollars. The Devil has Ivy Lee to thank for whatever damage Billy did to him, which probably was not very much. My personal opinion is that Billy Sunday set Christianity back a thousand years. They died about the time Ivy Lee passed on.

Rudolph Valentino (the late silent movie star, in case you have forgotten him) danced up and down Broadway, at a few dollars per dance, until a moving picture director discovered him and promoted him with media exposures. Then Valentino became the screen's great lover. The women of America, in the slang of the street, "ate it up!" When the talkies came all the stars of the silents had to be replaced overnight because most of them had no real ability in talking parts. The great lovers of the silents were great only because they had been cleverly promoted as such. The talkies proved that!

When the late Theodore Roosevelt came back from Africa, just after he left the White House in 1909, he made his first public appearance at the Madison Square Garden. Before he would agree to make the appearance he carefully arranged for nearly one thousand *paid applauders* to be scattered throughout the audience to applaud his entrance on the platform. For more than fifteen minutes these paid hand-clappers made the place ring with their enthusiasm. The other sheep took up the suggestion and joined in for another quarter hour. The newspaper men present nearly were literally swept off of their feet by the tremendous ovation given the American hero, and his name was emblazoned across the head-

lines of the newspapers in letters two inches high. Splendid! Teddy understood and made intelligent use of personal promotion. That was the
major reason why he was "a great statesman!"

One does not have to be an expert on propaganda or personal
promotion tactics to observe how effectively these forces were used by
Mussolini, Hitler, and Stalin, to maintain their standing in the eyes of the
world. They keep themselves constantly promoted in all sorts of favorable
lights because they know the necessity of appeasing home-folks and
impressing foreigners.

For a great number of years I served as my own business and promotion manager, yet I saw other men in my field going by me in an ever-
increasing line of procession. **I now know the habit of serving as
one's own promotion manager is something like the equally
foolish habit of cutting one's own hair. A man can cut his own
hair, but it does not improve his appearance. A man can also
serve as his own lawyer but he who does so usually follows his
own counsel into difficulty. There is no wisdom in following
such a course.**

Even a street can be made to take on a different reputation and yield
greater rents under the right sort of promotion direction. Fifth Avenue,
New York, is known the world over as the "highest class" street of
Manhattan. The reputation enables the owners of the ground to ask for
and receive fabulous rentals for their property. Fifth Avenue's reputation
is a promotion, maintained by the Fifth Avenue Association, through a
carefully managed promotion plan that keeps out the riff-raff which has
reduced Broadway and Forty-Second Street to nothing short of hunting
ground for mendicants and street peddlers. Stores on Broadway bring
but a fraction of the rentals received on Fifth Avenue.

Alvin York was merely another illiterate Tennessee mountaineer who
objected to conscription during the World War. He put up such a howl
about his "conscientious objection" that he attracted much attention
and plenty of newspaper space. After his return from war he was still
illiterate, but a clever little promoter took him over and now he dominates
a large school for mountain folks which was promoted in his name, the
State of Tennessee has dedicated one of its main highways to him, and

he has received financial and other forms of aid from influential people form all over the country. Verily, it pays to be properly *promoted*.

Thousands of Catholic Priests throughout America have never been heard of outside of their own parishes. Father Coughlin, self-promoter-extraordinary, made himself and his influence felt all over the country, and to some extent all over the world. He shone for a little while, then his candle flickered out. Father Coughlin could not, or did not take counsel from promotion experts. He talked himself into the limelight and out again. Under promotion management such as the late Ivy Lee, Father Coughlin would have become one of the political and economic factors which this country would have been compelled to heed.

I wonder how may readers of these lines know or ever heard of America's greatest thinker? I venture a guess that not half a dozen people could name him. He lives in Dallas, Texas, practices law, and his name is Stuart Austin Weir. He is, in my opinion, the most suitable man in the United States as the successor to Franklin D. Roosevelt. I doubt that there is living, in the world today, any person who has the depth and balance of thought that Mr. Weir possesses, and I doubt seriously that any philosopher, from Socrates to Elbert Hubbard, ever possessed the flexibility of thought, the variety of knowledge, the balance of judgement possessed by Weir. But Weir is practically unknown because he does not choose to avail himself of professional promotion service. Remember the name. You may hear it again. If you do it will be for the reason that someone who has a penchant for uncovering and publicizing men with brains, has voluntarily smoked Weir out into the open where the world can take a look at him.

Mrs. Franklin D. Roosevelt was not known as "the President's wife." She was known as herself. Professional promotion experts see to this! Whether or not this exploitation of Mrs. Roosevelt as an individual separate and distinct and independent from the President is good taste, it is not my business to say, but I do know that she is neither idle nor without income from her independent sources of service. One might think that a person as prominent as the wife of the president of the United States would not need professional promotion, but Mrs. Roosevelt is keen enough to know that no one is so big or important that he cannot be raised higher through well-organized promotion.

Now, how do these ideas apply in your case?

One of the major duties of life is that of selling one's way to some definite goal. **Not all of us are efficient promoters, therefore most of us need the services of experienced promotion experts who will assume the responsibility of keeping us steadily and favorably before the public.**

Over thirty years ago an enterprising young lawyer by the name of Paul Harris, in Chicago, conceived the brilliant idea of circumventing the rule against a lawyer advertising. He gathered around him thirty or so of his business friends and organized the first Rotary Club, the idea being, of course, to promote himself into a variety of contacts which might conceivably be converted into clients as the result of his personal relationship with them once a week. Today the Rotary Club movement has spread all over the world and has become an international power for good. The movement did its founder no harm!

Doctors, dentists, lawyers, architects, and other professional men whose professional ethics make direct advertising of themselves inadvisable might well profit by Paul Harris' example. Ethics is one thing, building up a professional practice is another! The two can be made to harmonize. That is the business of expert promotion men. And that goes for the rest of us as well.

> **If we wish to get ahead in the world we must find ways and means of bringing ourselves to the attention of people who need whatever we have to offer the world. Building a better mousetrap than one's neighbor will avail one nothing unless sound, intense, and continuous sales promotion is placed in support of the trap.**

Ham actors walk hungrily up and down Broadway, *trying to sell themselves*. Once in a blue moon a Ziegfeld discovers a Cantor, or a Will Rogers, or a Fanny Brice, and promotes him or her to the top, but blue moons do not rise often. The better plan is not to wait for "discovery," no matter who you are or what you have to offer the world. The better plan is to search until you find the one person best equipped to market the sort of services you have to offer, then give that person a good block of stock in yourself and tell him to go ahead and promote you!

While I was writing this story my doorbell rang. My visitor was a young man who had been acknowledged in America and abroad as one of the coming musical composers and pianist. He spent two hours trying to convince me there is virtue in the old habit of an artist starving in an attic rather than commercialize his art. He tried conscientiously enough to convince me that the philosophy of opulence, as outlined in my book, *Think and Grow Rich*, was an insult to great artists whose major business, from his view point, should be a willingness to starve for their art. I liked the young fellow. He had a pleasing personality, a brilliant mind, and a truly great passion for classical music. But I also felt very sorry for him— sorry because I knew his warped view of life would cost him his much coveted goal, the desire to be recognized as a truly great musician. He is already a great artist, but the world does not know him. Unless he allies himself with a set of brains skilled in marketing his services he may go through life an unknown genius, than which there is no greater tragedy.

The irony of this story is—the genius of whom I write came to my apartment to pick up a cast-off suit and overcoat I had promised him! Great heavens, this genius accepting alms merely because he does not believe in professional promotion.

A little while ago I was in the office of one of the editors of a syndicated service, with my manager, negotiating for the sale of some of my works. He told me that every well-known man in the literary field reached the top through clever promotion. He mentioned, in particular, the late Dr. Frank Crane, who wrote, in a light vein, a daily column for the newspapers. "When Dr. Crane first came to us," said this distinguished editor, "he was peddling his stuff here and there wherever he could get a country weekly newspaper to buy it, not earning enough to keep him and his family." I happen to know that when Dr. Crane died he was paying an income tax on upwards of $75,000.00 annually, all of this made from the sale of that same light vein column, marketed by an expert promotion man.

Elbert Hubbard made a sizeable fortune by writing and marketing his own works, but the world seldom knows more than one Elbert Hubbard at a time. He was one of those very rare persons who have the ability to create and to market the products of their creation. Most of us are lucky if we have the ability to *create*, much less sell our products.

I spent a quarter of a century organizing the philosophy of individual achievement. I wrote into that philosophy all that had been retrieved from the experiences of such men as Andrew Carnegie, Henry Ford, Thomas A. Edison, John Wanamaker, and others of their type, yet I found myself outmoded by the men who wrote books which they had thrown together overnight, as far as financial income was concerned. I finally awakened to myself, placed myself under management of my wife, and duty impels me to admit that I accomplished more in the way of recognition, during the first year of her management, than I had accomplished during all my previous years, while serving as my own manager.

> **It is each person's duty and responsibility to provide himself with whatever form of media promotion needed to help him attain success in his chosen calling.**

An unknown writer of verse expressed the thought beautifully in these lines—

> "It isn't strange that Princes and Kings,
> And clowns that caper in sawdust rings,
> And common folks like you and me,
> Are builders for eternity?
> To each is given a bag of tools,
> A shapeless mass and a book of rules,
> And each must make 'ere life has flown,
> A stumbling-block or stepping stone."

Self-advancement cannot be built on bluff, fear, or flattery!

Life demands of the successful man sterner stuff than these. Mere words and fine platitudes will never take the place of a practical plan doggedly put into action. And this, despite the fact that a book recently published was purchased by nearly a million people—in which the central theme admonished the reader to flatter those whom he wished to sway and attract.

A book on flattery may be helpful to those willing to stoop to flattery, but what of the "flatterees"—those unfortunates on whom the million purchasers of the book will work their magic? Are they to be deprived of protection against these seductive flatterers?

Personally, I resent all attempts of people to flatter me. If I used flattery in my work I would be instantly pegged as a charlatan, and rightfully so. I get better results by frankness in my dealings with people, for I find that direct, straight dealing not only *wins* friends, but also it *holds* them!

The greatest asset I have or shall ever have is a friend I won, not by flattery, but through the most scrutinizing analysis. That friend is my wife. I won her, not by telling her she was pretty, or smart, or witty. On the contrary I called her attention to all her weaknesses and suggested how she might correct them—*by marrying me!*

Morons and nit-wits like to be flattered, there is no denying that fact. People think or make any real pretense of thinking, resent all forms of flattery. It is an insult to their intelligence.

When anyone starts to flatter you it is a sure indication that person wants something you possess or some favor from you. Flattery is a form of "dope" which side tracks the reasoning faculty of the one flattered, and while it may, and often does permit the flatterer to gain temporary advantages, the time comes when the effect wears off and the victim comes out from under the spell with resentment in his heart.

The most that can be said of flattery is that it is sometimes a cheap psychological trick with which charlatans and dishonest people lull others into a state of carelessness while they pick their pockets. Flattery is the chief tool of all confident men. Through its use crooked stock salesmen take millions of dollars away from men and women annually. Through its use vicious spies wriggle their way into the confidence of military men and wheedle information from them.

Gold-diggers and women of questionable morals use flattery as a weapon with which to break down the resistance of men who will not respond to mere sex appeal. It is said that one highly publicized show girl, who has been married many times, managed to pick a millionaire every time she married because she is adept at the art of flattery. *But the marriages did not last!* Nothing built on flattery can last, for flattery is a weapon for ensnaring people designed and executed by the Devil.

The person who permits himself to be influenced by flattery is whipped before the battle begins. Samuel Insull's downfall really began when he started to pay more attention to the flattery of Grand Opera and opera stars than he gave to his business.

Some executives demand an affiliate of "yes men" around them. They would be safer if they employed a staff of "no men!" The human ego is a tricky piece of mental equipment. It needs constant protection against all forms of flattery, the one element to which an ego responds most readily.

One of the commonest mistakes is that of seeking a counsel of friends, even though they have been properly "influenced and won." The reason is that most so-called friends would rather flatter than be frank. They do not wish to offend, therefore their opinions are usually worth much less than the cost, because these opinions are generally misleading.

Movie stars and other quick-money victims shine for a time and then flicker out, mainly because they blow up and burst by feeding too freely on public flattery.

It is said that John W. Davis is paid an enormous sum annually by the J. P. Morgan banking firm, not for what he tells the members of the firm they can do, but for what he tells them they cannot do. He is the official *"no-man"* of the firm. He does no flattering to "win and influence" the Morgan partners. Astute businessmen that they are, they prefer cold facts to flattery. Perhaps this is why the Morgan firm is tops in the financial world.

Al Smith climbed from the fish market to within a stone's throw of the White House. His greatest help was Mrs. Bell Moscovics, his official *"no-woman".* It is no mere coincidence that the Brown Derby began to decline when Mrs. Moscovics died. Men who love to be flattered need immunity against this form of malady, and the ones who really think see that they get it.

Truly great business leaders do not depend upon flattery to get results. They have a better formula. Andrew Carnegie did not flatter Charles M.

Schwab. He got more dependable results by paying Mr. Schwab as high as a million dollars a year for his brains and his personality, *demanding loyalty and getting it!*

The Train Dispatcher does not flatter the conductor. He gives the conductor definite orders which he does not question. Once in awhile the orders may be neglected, then a wreck costs the conductor his job—or his life.

There are times when one should say "yes" and times when one should say "no." The author of a recent best-seller who advised her readers, as one of "The Twelve Disciplines," to say yes to all questions asked them for one whole day, could have been deeply embarrassed had she literally followed her own counsel. Life is made up of situations and circumstances calling for "yeses" and "noes." The person who negotiates his way through life successfully learns to use each in its proper place.

Lincoln kept bitter enemies as members of his cabinet because he needed frank analysis and criticism. Woodrow Wilson ousted Cabinet Members who did not agree with him. The difference in records of the two Presidents is very great, and it will become greater with time.

How far would a military man get in warfare if soldiers were managed by flattery?

Flattery would not help one very much with most policemen and taxi-cab drivers.

The person who makes himself indispensable to others by rendering more service and better service than he is paid to render will accomplish more permanent results of a desirable nature than he could accomplish with all the flattery in the world.

If you would sell your way through life successfully look around you, see what useful service you can render to as many people as possible, make yourself of value to others, and you will not need to learn the art of flattery in order to win people and use personal influence. Moreover, those whom you do win will stay won!

To be well liked gives one great advantages, but flattery is not the tool with which this desirable end may be attained and held. A Pleasing Personality is worth a king's ransom to those who possess it, but such a personality is not developed through speaking honied words of flattery which mean nothing. A Pleasing Personality consists of 21 different

Employers are always on the lookout for a man or woman who does a better job of any sort than is customary, whether it be wrapping a package, writing a letter, or closing a sale.

characteristics which can be developed. You will find the complete description of these 21 assets in a subsequent chapter. Master them and make them your own property, then you will be able to *attract* and *hold* friends.

There are practical and tried rules for *attracting* and *holding friends!* You will find them all in the subsequent chapters of this book. These are not the rules used to gain temporary advantages over others. They are the rules gleaned from the life-work of Abraham Lincoln, Benjamin Franklin, Thomas Paine, Thomas Jefferson, Samuel Adams, Richard Henry Lee, George Washington, and half a hundred other truly great men who laid the very foundation of this country. They are the rules used also by the most successful business and industrial leaders the country has produced, such men as Andrew Carnegie, Thomas A. Edison, Henry Ford, Owen D. Young, Cyrus H. K. Curtis, Frank A. Vanderlip, and John Wanamaker.

If any of these men had advocated flattery as a means of getting ahead in the world I would have been impressed by their recommendation, but not one of them used or recommended so low and vulgar a method as a means of self-advancement.

When flattery and direct frankness are placed side by side the latter will win over the former nine hundred and ninety-nine times out of every thousand. Every truly great trial lawyer knows that attempts to flatter the jury are always fraught with definite hazards to his case. The most successful lawyers are those who deal with *facts* instead of relying upon flattery. The same is true of successful business executives. How far, for example, do you believe one would get by trying to influence Henry Ford through flattery?

If I appear to be over-emphasizing the importance of guarding against the dangers of relying upon flattery as a means of selling one's way through life it is because of the possible effects upon the large number of people who have been taught to use flattery as the hub of the wheel of personal advancement. I believe that philosophy is dangerous to all who embrace it, and especially is it hazardous to the young person just starting out, with little or no experience in the business world.

There are sound and commendable ways of winning friends and influencing people, through appeal based upon some combination of the

Nine Basic Motives described in another chapter. If you wish to climb to the top of the ladder of success and remain there it will be much safer to use these nine motives as the rungs of your ladder instead of depending upon flattery.

Every move, every act, and every thought of every human being of sound body and mind, who has reached the age of reason, is influenced by one or more of the Nine Basic Motives. When you come to the description of these motives study it carefully and learn how to influence people by genuine appeal to natural motives. Then you will experience no resentment from those whom you influence.

Success in any calling is largely a matter of one's being able to negotiate his way through life with a minimum amount of friction in connection with his relationship with other people. By mastering, understanding, and applying the Nine Basic Motives you may reduce misunderstandings, opposition from others, and friction, to a minimum. Do this and you will be a great salesman, no matter what may be your calling.

Lest all this counsel impress you as a mere preachment. I am taking a liberty in citing at least one illustration of a circumstance in connection with which practical application was made of the principles of salesmanship recommended in the philosophy of personal negotiation.

At the end of the first year of the world depression I found myself divested of my money and most of my worldly property. People were not interested in books, they were interested in eating. I closed my New York office and moved to Washington, D. C., where I planned to remain until the economic storm had passed.

Months stretched out into years and instead of the depression passing it became worse. Finally I reached a decision not to wait for the end of the business stagnation, but to go on the lecture platform and work my way back into useful service to others who, also, had been wounded.

I decided to make my start in Washington. For this purpose I needed newspaper space for advertising. The amount of space I required would cost over two thousand dollars and I did not have this amount, neither could I get it from the usual banking sources. Here I was face to face with a situation similar to that which you and every other person on earth must sometime experience. *I was in need of something I had to procure with mere words.*

Here, then, is a brief description of exactly what I did and said in order to surmount my problem:

I went to Colonel Leroy Heron, Advertising Director of the *Washington Star*, and made known to him my needs. In approaching him I had two courses available to me. I could flatter him or I could tell him what a great paper he represented, what a fine record he made in the World War, what a great advertising man I believed him to be, and all that sort of piffle. Or, I could lay all my cards on the table and tell him what I wanted, why I wanted it, and why I believed I should get it. I chose the latter method of approach.

Then I was forced to decide whether I would disclose to Colonel Heron *all* the facts, including my financial weakness, or skip over these embarrassing subjects without clearly discussing them.

Again I chose to rely upon frankness and directness. There come times in one's life, when no other plan will secure the desired results.

As well as I can remember, here is a word for word statement of what I said:

"Colonel Heron, I wish to use the Washington Star in an advertising campaign to announce a series of public lectures on the philosophy of individual achievement. The space I require will amount to approximately $2500.00. My problem is in the unpleasant fact that I do not have that amount of money available. I had that amount and more a short time ago, but the depression consumed it.

"My request for credit is based upon the usual commercial credit rating. On that basis I would not be entitled to the credit. My appeal is based upon the fact (plenty of evidence of which I am prepared to present to you here and now) that I have devoted a quarter of a century to the study of the principles of individual achievement. During this time I have had the active cooperation of such men as Andrew Carnegie, Thomas A. Edison, Frank A. Vanderlip, John Wanamaker, and Cyrus H. K. Curtis. These men thought enough of me to give freely of their time and experience, over a long period of years, while I was organizing the philosophy of success. The time each gave to me was worth many times the amount of credit I am asking of you. Through their cooperation, I am now prepared to take to the world a philosophy of self-help, which all the people of the world badly need. If you do not wish to extend me the credit as a sound business risk, then extend it in the same spirit of helpfulness that these men of affairs gave to me of their time and experience."

The credit was extended to me by Colonel Heron on my brief statement of my case, with this significant remark:

"I do not know what your chances are of paying for the space you want but I believe I know enough of human nature to understand that you intend to pay for the space. I also believe that any philosophy organized from the life work of such men as Edison and Carnegie is sound and needed at this time. Moreover, I believe anyone to whom these men would devote their priceless time is worthy of much more credit than you seek with the Star. Bring in your copy and I will run it. We will talk to the credit manager afterward."

After the transaction had been completed and the advertising paid for I called on Colonel Heron again and had a very intimate personal talk with him. I asked him to tell me frankly why he extended the credit in face of the fact I had told him all about my financial weakness and nothing whatsoever of my ability to pay the account.

His reply was illuminating! "I gave you the credit," he exclaimed, "because you made no attempt to cover up your financial weakness. You resorted to no subterfuge and did not set your best foot forward first."

How far do you suppose I would have gotten had I appealed to Colonel Heron on anything but frankness?

The old-time salesman carried with him a supply of cigars, good liquor, and burlesque stories with which to entertain his prospective buyers. All these have been supplanted by motion pictures and highly colored graphs and charts with which the salesman can paint in the mind of his prospective buyer a perfect picture of the merchandise he sells.

There are nine windows and doors through which the human mind can be entered and influenced. Not one of these is labeled "flattery." The nine doors are the Nine Basic Motives by which all people are influenced.

Remember, as you read and digest the contents of this book that it is not a book on flattery. It is not a book of pleasantries and platitudes. It is not a book on psychological tricks and legerdemain. But, it is a book based on the recorded *facts and realities of life as they have been organized from experiences of the most able leaders the country has ever produced.*

*   *   *   *   *

"Seek counsel of men who will tell you the truth about yourself, even if it hurts you to hear it. Mere commendation will not help bring the improvement you need."

– Napoleon Hill

*   *   *   *   *

CHAPTER 3
The Strategy of
Master Salesmanship

*M*otive is the seed from which a sale may be germinated. All seed must contain the life germ or it will not germinate, regardless of the kind of soil in which it is planted. *Motive*, too, must contain the life germ or it will not germinate into a *sale*. The man who understands how to inject the "germ of life" into *motive* is a Master Salesman—*a master because he captures prospective buyer's own imagination and makes it work for him!*

When an appropriate motive has been painted in the mind of the prospective buyer by a *real artist*, it begins to work from within as yeast works in a loaf of bread. Let us illustrate this point, viz:

The late Dr. Harper, while servicing as president of the University of Chicago, *desired* to construct a new building on the campus, the estimated cost of which was $1,000,000.00. His available funds were not sufficient for his needs, nor did he see any chance of securing the necessary funds from the university's annual budget. After analysis of the situation, it became apparent to Dr. Harper that he would have to seek out the million dollars from an outside source.

Here begins the description of the modus operandi of a Master Salesman.

Dr. Harper *did not* start buttonholing wealthy men for donations. He did not put on a "drive" for donations. He made up his mind to get the entire sum through a single sale; moreover, he assumed personally the responsibility for making the sale.

> **His first move was to *lay out a plan of action!* (here is where most people fail. . . because they lack a plan that is definite and sound.)**

His plan when completed involved only two prospective donors. From one or the other he intended to secure the needed funds. His plan was conceived with ingenuity and rounded out with strategy—keen, penetrating strategy, which was alive and filled with *lure!* It was also loaded with dynamite. What did he do?

He chose, as his two prospective donors, two Chicago millionaires whom he knew to be *bitter enemies.* Yes, yes, I know. You are beginning to see the point before it has been explained. But follow on and get the technique of a Master Sales Artist.

One of these men was the head of the Chicago Street Railway system. The other was a politician who had accumulated a great fortune by "gouging" the streetcar company and by other methods.

Dr. Harper's selection of "prospective buyers" of his plan was perfect. (Here again is a point at which all but Master Artists at Selling are usually weak. They do not use sound judgement in the selection of "prospective buyers".)

After turning his plan over in his mind for a few days, and carefully rehearsing his sales presentation, Dr. Harper swung into *action!*

Choosing the noon hour as the most favorable for his call, he presented himself at the office of the streetcar magnate. Observe with profit *his reason* for choosing this particular hour. He deduced that the executive's secretary would be at lunch at that hour and that his prospect would be alone in his office. His deduction proved to be sound. Finding the outer office empty, he walked on into the private office. The magnate looked up at the intruder in surprise and asked, "What can I do for you, sir?"

"I beg your pardon for the intrusion," Dr. Harper replied, "I am Dr. Harper, President of the University of Chicago. I found no one in the outer office, so I took the liberty of walking in."

"Why, yes, of course," the other exclaimed, "have a seat Dr. Harper. I am glad to have the honor of your visit."

"Thank you," the Doctor replied, "I am in a great hurry and will stand, if you don't mind. I just dropped in to tell you of an idea that has been running in my mind for some time. (Here comes the *motive*. Watch how deftly it is planted in fertile soil.) First of all, I want to tell you how greatly I admire the wonderful system of street railway transportation you have given the people of Chicago. (Neutralizing his "prospect's mind.) I believe it to be the greatest system in the country. It has occurred to me, however, that while you have built a great monument to your name, it is of such a nature that the world will forget who built it the moment you die. (Watch the Master go back now to the *motive*.)

"I would like to see you build a monument that will endure forever. I have thought of a plan by which you might build such a monument, but I have met with some difficulties which, I am sorry to say, may stand in the way. (Pulling the *"lure"* away from the prospect to make the idea more desirable.) I had thought of securing for you the *privilege* of constructing a beautiful granite building on the University campus, but some members of our Board want this privilege to go to Mr. X (mentioning the name of the political enemy). I am holding out in your favor and just came by to ask if you can think of any plan that may help me to secure this rare privilege for you."

"That is most interesting!" the magnate exclaimed. "Please sit down and let us talk about the matter."

"I am exceedingly sorry," Dr. Harper replied, "but we are having a Board meeting in an hour and I must hurry along. If you think of an argument I might use in your behalf, please telephone me as promptly as possible and I will go to bat for you before the Board. Good day, sir."

Dr. Harper turned and walked out. When he reached his office, he found that the streetcar magnate had already telephoned him three times requesting that Dr. Harper call him as soon as he came in.

The Doctor was obliging. He telephoned the magnate, who requested that he be permitted to come out and present his case to the Board in person. Dr. Harper replied that this would be inadvisable; that in view of the opposition some of the Board members had expressed toward him, Dr. Harper might present the matter more "diplomatically," (*Intensifying* the *lure*.)

"If you will telephone me tomorrow morning," Dr. Harper suggested, "I will let you know what luck I have had."

The next morning upon arriving at his office, he found the streetcar magnate already there. They were closeted together for half an hour. What happened probably will never be known to the public. The interesting thing, however, is that *the street car magnate assumed the role of salesman, while Dr. Harper became the "buyer" and was "persuaded" to accept a check for a million dollars and to promise that he would try to get it accepted by the Board!*

The check was accepted!

What arguments Dr. Harper used with his Board no one knows, but the million dollar building now stands on the campus of the University, silent but impressive evidence that mastery in selling is never accidental. The building bears the name of the donor.

Hearing of this incident, I called Dr. Harper and asked him to tell me why some of the members of his Board should prefer to honor a racketeering politician. In reply, he merely shrugged his shoulders and smiled at me, a queer little twinkle in his eyes. *His answer was sufficient.* I got the idea. The opposition existed mainly in Dr. Harper's imagination. To place the transaction in the category of "justified strategy," Dr. Harper probably developed the idea of friendly opposition in the minds of some of the members of his Board.

Let us analyze this transaction to make sure that the fine points are not overlooked. First of all, observe that *no high-pressure methods* were used by Dr. Harper. He depended entirely upon *motive* to turn the trick for him. No doubt he spent days planning his approach. Incidentally, the *motive*, which he chose, is one of the most alluring of all the motives. In fact, he made his appeal through two motives, namely:

(a) **The motive of** *desire for fame and power*
   and
(b) **The motive of** *revenge*

The street car magnate saw instantly that he could perpetuate his name in the role of public benefactor in such a way that it would go marching on long after his remains had gone back to dust, and his street railway system had, perhaps, been supplanted by some other mode of travel. He saw also (Thanks to Dr. Harper's sound strategy) an opportunity to get *revenge* on his bitterest enemy by depriving him of the privilege of a great honor.

No great amount of imagination is required to enable one to see what would have happened if Dr. Harper had made his approach in the usual manner: by writing a letter to the street car magnate asking for an appointment, thus giving him an opportunity to anticipate the *motive* behind the request. Any one but a Master Salesman would have made the approach either in this way or by presenting himself at the man's office and requesting him to "help the University out of a hole" by *giving* it a million dollars.

Suppose, for illustration, that Dr. Harper had not understood the psychology of *motive* and had not been a Master Salesman. He would have visited the magnate and this is about the way the conversation would have taken place:

"Good morning, sir. I am Dr. Harper, President of the University of Chicago. I have come to ask for a few minutes of your time. (Asking for favors to begin with, *instead of offering favors!* Failure to neutralize the prospective buyer's mind.) We need an extra million dollars for a new building which we intend to erect on the campus of the University, and I thought you might be interested in donating the amount. You have been successful. You have a great street railway system from which you earn big profits; profits which really have been made possible through the patronage of the public. Now it is only fair that you should show your appreciation of the success which the public has made possible for you by doing something for the public good."

Observe in your mind's eye this scene. The streetcar magnate is fidgeting in his chair and nervously fussing with some papers on his desk, groping for an alibi with which to refuse. As soon as the Doctor hesitates for a moment in his sales presentation, the magnate takes up the conversation.

"I am exceedingly sorry, Dr. Harper, but our budget for philanthropic purposes has been entirely exhausted. You know we make a liberal annual donation to the Community Chest fund. There is nothing more we can do this year. Besides, a million dollars is a large sum of money. I am sure our Board could not be persuaded to donate so much money to *charity*." (He beats the Doctor to that "Board" gag.)

That word *"Charity!"*

You see, of course, that a poor presentation would have placed Dr. Harper in the unhappy position of one who begs for charity. Giving to charity, as such, is not listed as one of the nine basic motives which move men to action. But lift the word "charity" out of its humble setting and give it the color of *privilege, fame,* and *honor* and it takes on an entirely different meaning. *Only a Master Salesman can do this.*

One way is clever; the other is crude.

The act of selling, if scientifically conducted, may be compared to an artist at his easel. Stroke by stroke, as the artist develops form and harmony and blends the colors on a canvas, the Master Salesman paints a *word picture* of the thing he is offering for sale. The canvas on which he paints is the *imagination* of the prospective buyer. He first roughly outlines the picture he wants to paint, later filling in the details, using *ideas* for paint. In the center of the picture, at the focal point, he draws a clearly defined outline of *motive!* As a painting on a canvas, must be based upon a *motive,* or theme, so must a successful sale.

The picture, which the Master Sales Artist paints in the mind of his prospective buyer, must be more than a mere skeleton outline. Details must be perfected so the prospect not only sees the picture in perspective as a finished whole, but the picture must be pleasing to him! *Motive* is the one thing that determines how pleasing the picture can be made.

Amateurs and little children may draw a rough picture of a horse, which can be recognized to be the picture of a horse. But when the Master Artist draws a picture of a horse, those who see it not only recognize it as a horse but exclaim, "How wonderful! How lifelike!!" The artist paints action, reality, and life into his picture!

There is the same difference between men who call themselves sales-men and a Master Salesman as there is between the dabbler and the master painter. The inefficient salesman hurriedly sketches a crude out-line of the thing he wishes to sell, leaving *motive* out of the picture. He says, "See? There it is, as plain as the nose on your face! Now will you buy?" But the prospective buyer *does not see* that which the salesman has kept hidden within his own mind. Or he may "see" but does not *feel.* He is not moved to *action* by any rough sketch or unfinished, lifeless picture. No seed of *desire* has been planted in his mind; no appeal to *motive.*

That's why he doesn't get desired results.

The Master Salesman paints another picture. He omits no detail. He mixes word-colorings so that they blend with harmony and symmetry, which capture his prospective buyer's

imagination. He builds the picture around a motive which dominates the entire scene, putting the prospective buyer's own mind to work in his behalf. That is Master Salesmanship!

A little while ago a great artist came to sell me life insurance. As everyone knows, life insurance is an abstract, intangible and one of the hardest things in the world to sell. One cannot see it; one cannot smell it, or taste it, or feel it, or "sense" it through any of the five senses. In addition to these handicaps, one must in a sense and under certain conditions, *die in order to profit by it.* Even then the profit goes to someone else.

No amateur is a successful life insurance salesman!

But this artist was no amateur. Through study and preparation, he had gained the status of a Master. He had familiarized himself with the *motives* which most quickly and effectively appeal to the prospective purchaser of life insurance. He had prepared himself to analyze his prospective buyers accurately in order that he might readily catalog them as to the *motive* best suited to each case.

> **He placed before my eyes an invisible canvas, and on this canvas, with only words for brushes and paints, he drew a picture of *me* twenty years hence, with shoulders drooping and fast-graying hair. Around me he grouped my family. In this picture he transformed my wife from a women of youth and vigor, beauty, and independence, into an aging, *dependent* person! He played upon my heartstrings through that word *dependent*, as a master violinist would play upon the strings of a Stradivarius. Nor was the picture yet complete. He added another scene in which I saw myself lying cold in death! I felt shivers running down my spine as the artist played upon that word *death!* (Reaching me through the motive of *fear*, one of the strongest of the nine basic motives.) By my coffin was my wife, a helpless dependent old woman; the woman whom I knew I loved and whose future he knew I would want to make secure. (Reaching me through the motive of *love*, another of the nine basic motives.)**

Only an artist can paint such a picture. It was so realistic that it still haunts me!

I took that picture to bed with me that night. It was a nightmare that caused me to groan and turn from side to side, seeking to escape its horror. In sleep my sub-conscious mind seized upon it and tortured me with terrible dreams. (By planting in it the motive of fear, the salesman had made a friendly ally of my mind.)

Only an artist can paint such a picture, yet artists are *made*, not born! They may be born with the inherent potentialities for artistic creation, but they become finished artists only by mastering the technique of harmony, form, and color. Sales artists, too, are *made* and not born. They become masters by studying technique and motive; they develop expert methods of analyzing buyers and the things they buy.

Dr. Harper was not a "born salesman." He was small in physique and unprepossessing in appearance. He became a great salesman by studying men and the *motives* which cause men to act. That is exactly what all who would attain to mastery in selling must do. The old bromide about salesmen being "born and not made" is as weak as it is old. The 30,000 salesmen whom I have trained have taught me that salesmen can be made.

I have had the privilege of knowing intimately perhaps as many as a hundred Master Salesman during my day as an educator of salesmen; most of the others in the sales field whom I have known, numbering well into the thousands, have been just plain order takers.

The difference in earning capacity between a Master Salesman and an order taker is very great. It runs all the way from several thousand dollars to as much as a million dollars a year. The late John W. Gates earned a million dollars a year with much less effort than most salesmen earning $3,000.00. He was an artist. The late "Diamond" Jim Brady had no difficulty in converting his talents into a like amount of money. He, too, was a master. These two men (and all others in their class) used showmanship and technique and method where most salesmen depend upon shoe leather instead of technique and method.

Master Salesmanship consists of a series of picture impressions which are deftly painted in the mind of the prospective buyer through one or more of the five senses. If these word-pictures are not clear and distinct, beautifully

harmonized and properly fertilized with *motive*, they will not move the prospective buyer to action.

Master Salesmen paint their pictures in the minds of their prospective buyers through as many motives and through as many of the senses as possible. They often supplement mere word pictures with samples or actual pictures of their wares. They know that sales are more easily made when the presentation reaches the mind of the prospective buyer through more than one of the five senses and also when more than one motive for buying has been planted in the buyer's mind.

Master Salesmanship begins and ends with proper motive! As long as the right motive has been injected into the selling argument, it makes very little difference what happens between the opening and closing of a sale.

All selling is like this, in a way. Men are moved to buy or not to buy because of motive! Base your sales presentation upon the right motive and your sale is made before you start.

Remember, however, that motive usually must be established in the mind of the prospective buyer; that most people have neither the imagination nor the inclination to build their own motives for *your* wares. Only a weak-willed person will permit himself to be *sold* unless a sufficiently impelling motive has been tactfully but forcefully planted in his mind by the salesman.

Showmanship **is not only one of the important factors in Master Salesmanship, but it is important in practically every other calling.**

An efficient showman is one who can dramatize the commonplace events of life and give them the interesting appearance of uniqueness. Efficient showmanship calls for sufficient imagination to be able to recognize things, people, and circumstances, which are capable of being dramatized.

Through the aid of efficient showmanship, Roger Babson has made a fortune out of dry statistics and monotonous columns of figures. Through the use of graphic charts and appropriate illustrations, he has literally made figures talk. His success is due almost if not entirely to his showmanship ability.

Theodore Roosevelt was one of the most colorful Presidents who ever occupied the White House, although many doubt that he was one of the most brilliant or capable executives. He was popular because he was a master showman and understood publicity and dramatic values, and made use of both effectively.

Perhaps Calvin Coolidge had the least colorful personality of any man who ever occupied the White House. He appeared frigid and reserved. Theodore Roosevelt was vital and enthusiastic. Moreover, he understood how to display his magnetism. Roosevelt will be remembered and talked about long after the "Mayor of Northampton" has been forgotten, because he knew how to dramatize the commonplace and prosaic events of life so they would stand out and attract attention. Great personalities are remembered.

People buy personalities and ideas much more quickly than they buy merchandise. For this very reason the salesman who is an efficient showman may make sales where other salesmen cannot. The life insurance salesman, who knows nothing about showmanship and does not possess a magnetic personality, usually tail-ends the list of producers. The life insurance salesman, who is an efficient showman and possesses a magnetic personality, sells everything except statistics and seldom mentions the word "policy." He does not have to. He deals in ideas, and uses them to paint alluring pictures, which interest and please his prospective buyers.

An efficient showman makes effective use of *enthusiasm*. The poor showman knows nothing of enthusiasm. He trusts his case to his own colorless statements of fact, which he intends as an appeal to the prospective buyer's reason. **Most people are not influenced largely by reason; they are swayed by *emotion*, or feeling. The man who is not capable of arousing his own emotions very deeply is not apt to be able to appeal to others through their emotional nature.**

During the heyday of his career, Bill Sunday was the greatest showman who ever went gunning for the Devil. He could sell tickets into heaven and make the crowds stand in line and like it. The public paid him millions of dollars while other preachers, who lacked a sense of the

To become a master salesman you must daily engage in study time, reading time, thinking time, and planning time.

dramatic, starved to death. Had Sunday been selling patent medicine instead of tickets through the Pearly Gates, he would have been arrested.

Be an able salesman and you can be almost anything else you wish to be.

Jimmie Walker was an efficient showman, however poor a mayor he may have been. Ex-Mayor James F. Hylan was, perhaps, one of the best mayors New York City ever had and the least capable in showmanship. The difference in their popularity was the difference between showmanship and the lack of it!

Will Rogers made himself popular through his comments on the highlights of world news because he had a sufficient sense of the dramatic to make his remarks fit people's moods. That is not only showmanship, it is salesmanship of the highest order.

Arthur Brisbane was the highest paid newspaper columnist in America. His yearly income was well above half a million dollars. He made a fortune through his "Today" column because of his ability to dramatize what people think about, or what they want to think about, and to color the news of the day.

The Sales Manager who is not an efficient showman is defeated before he begins. He must bring out showmanship qualities in his salesmen.

A sales presentation, delivered by an able showman, is a show all by itself and as interesting as a play. Moreover, it carries the prospective buyer through exactly the same mental processes that a good play does. A salesman who is an able showman can change the prospective buyer's mind from negative to positive at will. He can accomplish this change of mental attitude, not by accident or luck but by a carefully pre-arranged plan. An able showman can "neutralize" the mind of his prospective buyer regardless of the state of mind he may be in when approached, and what is more important, the able showman knows enough not to try to reach a climax or close his sale until this change has been successfully effected.

The farmer cannot raise wheat in paying quantities without preparation of the soil *before the seed is sown.* No more can a salesman plant the seed of desire in the prospective buyer's mind while that mind is negative. The salesman who understands showmanship prepares the mind of the prospective buyer as carefully and scientifically as the farmer prepares his ground. If he does not, he is not a salesman.

A little while ago, a salesman walked into a man's office while the man was engaged in a heated argument with his wife over the telephone. When the conversation was finished, the man turned to the salesman and barked, "What the hell do you want?" Undismayed by the unfortunate moment of his call, the salesman replied in a soft drawl and with a kindly grin, "I am organizing a Defense Club for husbands," going on to explain that he also had "that kind of wife." The two men talked about women for ten minutes, after which the salesman tactfully switched the talk to his own wares and went away with a $10,000.00 sale. That was showmanship plus salesmanship. The salesman who knew nothing about showmanship would have failed in this case. This salesman, knowing the value of the dramatic, turned an unfortunate situation into an advantage for himself.

William Burnette converted a plan of sales strategy into five million dollars in five years by teaching salesman how to sell *ideas* about kitchen utensils made of aluminum. His entire plan can be described in one sentence: He taught his salesman how to organize clubs for housewives, for the purpose of selling them aluminum ware.

More specifically, Burnette's plan was to invite the housewives of a community to a luncheon at one of their homes, all expenses to be paid for, and the meal cooked by one of his salesman with the aluminum ware he was selling. After the luncheon the salesman would take orders for the aluminum ware running all the way from twenty-five dollars to three times that amount.

It was the sales strategy of the plan that turned the trick for Burnette. Because he was a Master Salesman, William Burnette lifted himself from the lowly work of house-to-house canvassing in which he had previously been engaged to make himself a multimillionaire in five years.

Bear in mind the fact that his salesmen were selling a complete kitchen set of aluminum ware, not merely a few pots and pans. Also, no individual selling was done. The work consisted of group sales, which took place after the luncheon had been served. The women at whose home the luncheon was given usually signed the first order, the others quickly falling in line.

As the reader may observe, page after page of this book is devoted to emphasizing the importance of sales strategy or a plan which has been carefully built around the proper motive. One of the major differences between a Master Salesman and a sales "agent" is the fact that the Master Salesman is familiar with the nine basic motives and uses at least one of them as a foundation of his selling plan, while the sales "agent" uses neither motive nor plan. He tries to sell "main strength and awkwardness" through the hit or miss method which sometimes works but usually misses.

We shall soon describe the attributes of a Master Salesman, as well as the fundamental rules and principles of salesmanship. The preceding portion of this book has been intended to prepare the reader's mind to assimilate more quickly these rules and principles and to illustrate how they have been applied by men who have attained to mastery in selling.

In the next chapter we will describe the qualities which a Master Salesman must possess. In subsequent chapters we will describe how these qualities may be developed and how applied most effectively.

*   *   *   *   *

"If you can't forgive, don't ask to be forgiven."
– Napoleon Hill

*   *   *   *   *

CHAPTER 4
Qualities The Master Salesman Must Develop

There are many factors which enter into the equipment of the successful salesman. Most of these factors are personal in nature and have more to do with the salesman than with the goods or services he sells or the institution or organization he represents.

We will investigate these factors in detail.

In cultivating or inducing the principles here discussed, there are necessarily involved, first, a self-searching analysis to determine the presence or absence of these desirable qualities and, second, deliberate effort in cultivating them.

As most so-called mental traits have a physical basis, many of these desired qualities can be attained by doing or attempting to do those things which lead to a desired end. Science has abundantly proved that even a state of mind reflects a physical condition and that chemical and physical factors within the body itself bring about the moods and feelings and thoughts which academic psychology has in the past been reluctant to classify as purely "mental."

Even thought has been proven by scientists, including the great John B. Watson, to be intimately bound up with speech. Watson declares that thought is, in effect, inarticulate speech; and that thinking is but a highly organized physical activity.

Therefore, talk to yourself about the things you want to take root and grow in your mind and character. This is the very first step.

And it is a very profitable step, too.

The second is like unto the first in that it is a physical activity, also. The second consists in doing the thing that you would like to do. We learn by experience. After all, it is the greatest of all teachers. Habits can be cultivated, as well in the mind as in the body because both mind and body function on a physical plane.

Now then, what are some of the absolutely necessary things for the Master Salesman to have in his mental equipment?

There follows is a list of very desirable qualities, which almost any normal and reasonable person can come to possess and exercise. The list is long and perfection may be only slowly attained. Therefore, before entering into a detailed consideration of the things you would like to have your mind and body capable of doing, let's at once enumerate those which are absolutely necessary.

1. ***Physical fitness*** is of tremendous importance for the simple reason that neither the mind nor body can function well without it. Therefore, give attention to your habits of life, proper diet, healthful exercise and fresh air.

2. ***Courage*** must be the part of every man or woman who succeeds in any undertaking, especially that of selling in these trying times of intense competition after a devastating period of depression and discouragement.

3. ***Imagination*** is an absolute requirement of a successful salesman. He must anticipate situations and even objections on the part of his prospective customer. He must have such a lively imagination as to enable its operation to place him in sympathetic understanding with the position, needs, and objectives of his customer. He must almost literally stand in the other man's shoes. This takes real imagination.

4. ***Speech.*** The tone of voice must be pleasing. A high-pitched squeaky voice is irritating. Words half swallowed are hard to understand. Speak distinctly and enunciate clearly. A meek voice indicates a weak person. A firm, clean-cut, clear voice that moves with assurance and color, indicates an aggressive person with enthusiasm and aggressiveness.

5. ***Hard work*** is the only thing that will turn sales training and ability into money. No amount of good health, courage, or imagination is worth a dime unless it is put to work. The amount of pay a salesman gets is usually fixed by the amount of very hard, intelligent work that he actually puts out. Many people side-step this factor of success.

The above principles are simple. There is nothing unusual or impossible or even striking in them separately or collectively, unless perhaps it is the fact that most salesmen fail to possess one or more of these five primary requisites.

Some salesmen may work hard and even intelligently, using their imaginations well until they meet a succession of rebuffs and turn downs. It is here that the salesman with sand in his soul, stamina in his backbone, and courage in his heart comes right back and whips the salesman who hasn't these qualities, so courage is essential.

Then again, many salesmen have been known to possess courage, imagination, and hard work, yet by dissipation and bodily excesses handicap themselves so as to be physically unfit half the time to carry on their work.

Other qualifications considered by experienced sales managers as necessary in the equipment of successful salesman are listed below:

6. ***Knowledge of the merchandise he sells.*** The super-salesman analyzes carefully the merchandise or service which he sells and understands thoroughly every advantage which it embraces, because he knows that no salesman can sell successfully that which he, himself, does not understand and believe.

7. ***Belief in the merchandise or service.*** The super-salesman never tries to sell anything in which he does not have implicit confidence because he knows that his mind will "broadcast" his lack of confidence to the mind of the prospective buyer, regardless of what he may say about his wares.

8. ***Appropriateness of merchandise.*** The super-salesman analyzes both his prospective buyer and his needs and offers him only that which is appropriate to both. He never tries to sell a Rolls Royce to a man who ought to purchase a Ford,

even if the prospective buyer is financially able to buy the more expensive car. ***He knows a bad bargain for the buyer is a worse bargain for the seller!***

9. ***Value Given.*** The super-salesman never tries to get more for his wares than they are actually worth, realizing that the sustained *confidence* and *good-will* of his prospective buyer is worth more than a "long-profit" on a single sale.

10. ***Knowledge of the prospective buyer.*** The super-salesman is a character analyst. He has the ability to ascertain, from his prospective buyer, which of the nine basic motives he will respond to most freely, and he builds his sales presentation around those motives. Moreover, if his prospective buyer has no outstanding motive for buying, the super-salesman creates one for him, knowing that a motive is essential in "closing" a sale.

11. ***Qualifying the prospective buyer.*** The super-salesman never tries to make a sale until he has properly "qualified" the prospective buyer, thereby informing himself, in advance of his efforts to close on a sale, on the following points:

   (**a**) The prospective buyer's *financial* capacity to purchase
   (**b**) His *need* for that which is being offered for sale
   (**c**) His *motive* in making the purchase

   Endeavoring to make sales without first qualifying the prospective buyer is a mistake, which stands at the head of the list of causes of "no sale."

12. ***Ability to "neutralize" the mind of the buyer.*** The super-salesman knows that no sale can be made until the mind of the prospective buyer has been neutralized, or made receptive. Because he knows this, he will not endeavor to "close" a sale until he has "opened" the mind of the buyer and prepared it as a background or base upon which he may put together the word-mosaic of his story. This is the point where many salesmen fail.

13. ***Ability to close a sale.*** The super-salesman is an artist at reaching and successfully passing the closing point in selling. He trains himself to sense the psychological moment when

terminal facilities may be reached successfully. He rarely, if ever, asks the prospective buyer if he is ready to purchase. Instead, he goes on an assumption that the buyer is ready and conducts himself in a conversation and general demeanor accordingly. *Here he uses the power of suggestion most effectively.* The super-salesman avoids trying to close a sale until he knows in his own mind that he can close successfully. He so conducts his sales presentation that his prospective buyer believes he has done the buying.

Other principles to be acquired have more to do with the personal make-up and self-organization of the salesman than his goods. Some of these follow:

14. ***A pleasing personality.*** The super-salesman has acquired the art of making himself agreeable to other people because he knows that the prospective buyer must buy the salesman as well as the merchandise he sells or no sale can be made. (See the 21 factors of a pleasing personality, Chapter 14.)
15. ***Showmanship.*** The super-salesman is also a super-showman! He has the ability to reach the mind of his prospective buyer by dramatizing his presentation and by giving it "color" sufficient to arouse intense interest through an appeal to the prospective buyer's imagination.
16. ***Self-control.*** The super-salesman has *and exercises* complete control over his head and his heart, at all times, knowing that if he does not control himself, he cannot control his prospective buyer.
17. ***Initiative.*** The super-salesman understands the value, and uses the principle of initiative. He never has to be told what to do or how to do it. Having a keen imagination, he uses it and creates plans, which he translates into action, through his initiative. He needs but little supervision and, generally speaking, is given none.
18. ***Tolerance.*** The super-salesman is open-minded and tolerant on all subjects, knowing as he does that open-mindedness is essential for growth.

19. *Accurate thinking.* The super-salesman thinks! Moreover, he takes the time and goes to the trouble to gather *facts* as the basis of his thinking. He does no guessing when *facts* are available. He has no set or immovable opinions which are not based upon what he knows to be facts.

20. *Persistence.* The super-salesman is never influenced by the word "no" and he does not recognize the word "impossible." To him *all things are possible for achievement.* The word "no" to super-salesman is nothing more than a signal to begin his sales presentation in earnest. He knows that all buyers take the line of least resistance by resorting to the "no" alibi. Because he has this knowledge, he is not susceptible to negative influence by sales resistance.

21. *Faith.* The super-salesman has the capacity for "super-faith" in:

    (a) The thing he is selling
    (b) Himself
    (c) His prospective buyer
    (d) Closing the sale

Moreover, he never tries to make a sale without the aid of this faith because he knows that faith is contagious; that his faith is picked up through the "receiving station" of the prospective buyer's mind and acted upon as if it were the prospective buyer's own state of mind. Without the quality of faith there can be no super-salesmanship! Faith is a state of mind, which may be described as an intensified form of self-reliance. It is said that "faith moves mountains" but it also makes sales.

22. *Habit of observation.* The super-salesman is a close observer of small details. Every word uttered by the prospective buyer, every change of facial expression, every movement is observed and its significance weighed accurately. The super-salesman not only observes and analyzes accurately all that his prospective buyer does and says, but he also makes deductions from that which he *does not* do or say. Nothing escapes the super-salesman's attention!

23. ***The habit of rendering more service than is expected of him.*** The super-salesman follows the habit of rendering service which is greater in quantity and finer in quality than he is expected to render, thereby profiting by the law of Increasing Returns, as well as by the law of Contrast.

24. ***Profiting by failures and mistakes.*** The super-salesman experiences no such contingent as "lost effort." He profits by all of his mistakes and, through observation, by the mistakes of others. He knows that in every failure and mistake may be found (if analyzed) the seed of an equivilent success!

25. ***The master mind.*** The super-salesman understands and applies the "Master Mind" principle, through which he greatly multiplies his power to achieve. (The Master Mind principle means "the coordination of two or more individual minds, working in perfect harmony for a definite purpose.")

26. ***A definite major aim.*** The super-salesman works always with a *definite* sales quota, or goal, in mind. He never goes at his work merely with the aim of selling all he can. He not only works with a definite goal in mind, but he has a definite time in which to attain the object of that goal. The psychological effect of a definite chief aim will be described in the chapter on auto-suggestion.

27. ***The Golden Rule applied.*** The super-salesman uses the Golden Rule as the foundation of all his business transactions, putting himself in the "other man's shoes," and seeing the situation from his viewpoint. This quality will be a greater necessity in the future than it has been in the past because of the changes in business ethics, which have taken place as the result of the Business Depression.

Of all the qualities that a salesman must possess none is more necessary, none more valuable than the next one, which is:

28. ***Enthusiasm.*** The super-salesman has an abundance of enthusiasm, which he can use at will. Moreover, he knows

the vibrations of thought which he releases through his enthusiasm will be picked up by the prospective buyer and acted upon as if it were his own creation.

Enthusiasm is a difficult thing to explain, but its presence is always easily recognized. Everybody likes the enthusiastic person. He is high of spirit and radiates an atmosphere of good fellowship, high faith, and lofty purpose. Perhaps enthusiasm is born as much of his own deep faith in himself, the mission of work he carries on and the good he does in his work as anything. Enthusiasm in people and the lack of it may be compared to the light that surrounds a flashing diamond on a jeweler's tray with its spontaneity and iridescence which compel admiration and give value to it, and then the dull leaden atmosphere surrounding a piece of glass the same size. The glass can be bought for a song with none willing to sing it, while the diamond is eagerly sought by all, great and small, rich and poor.

Therefore, to every salesman this advice is given as though from Sinai:

With all thy getting, get enthusiasm.

Mastery in connection with these major factors in selling entitles those who sell to rate as super-salesman! Study the list carefully and make sure you are not weak in connection with any of these qualities if you aspire to mastery in selling.

Observe that every quality may be acquired!

This does not harmonize with the false notion held by some people that *"Salesmen are born and not made."* Salesmanship is an art and a science and maybe acquired by those with the will to acquire it! Some people are blessed with personalities that are favorable to quick mastery of the factors of super-salesmanship, while others must develop such a personality, but it can be developed.

THE NINE BASIC MOTIVES
TO WHICH PEOPLE RESPOND MOST FREELY

Science has catalogued the responses of which normal people are capable and has set forth for us the types of appeal which will induce desired responses.

Response may be of a low grade, such as scientists would call purely physical or which are prompted by physio-chemical stimuli. You may cause a man to get out of the office by kicking him out—that is purely physical—or he may be induced to act by reason of those chemical reactions incident to a peculiar condition of the physical body. Temperature, atmosphere, and physical comforts or discomforts, as well as foods and drink, bring about such chemical conditions as to prompt certain reactions.

> **But forgetting these more elementary and purely physical responses, we may classify the appeals that induce appropriate responses under three heads. These appeals are the only ones to which we need address ourselves in this study. They are:**
>
> **1. Appeals to instinct**
> **2. Appeals to emotion**
> **3. Appeals to reason**

The appeals, which cause most people to buy food, clothing and shelter, fall primarily into the first group, though in lesser degree they may find a field of expression in the other two.

All beautiful things in the world that are desirable because of their beauty may be sold because of suitable appeals made under the second heading: emotion.

Love, marriage, and religion deal largely in appeals that are emotional. Many goods and services are sold on emotional appeal. Education, books, the theater, music and art, life insurance, advertising, cosmetics, luxuries, toys, and a long list of things are all sold on emotional appeal.

Investments, savings, mechanical appliances, business machines, and scientific works often change hands on appeals to reason.

There are nine basic motives to which people respond and one by one or more of which they are influenced in practically every thought and deed. When the super-salesman qualifies his prospective buyers he looks first for the most logical motive with which he may influence their minds.

THE NINE BASIC MOTIVES

1. **The motive of self-preservation**
2. **The motive of financial gain**
3. **The motive of love**
4. **The motive of sex urge**
5. **The motive of desire for power and fame**
6. **The motive of fear**
7. **The motive of revenge**
8. **The motive of freedom (of body and mind)**
9. **The motive of desire to build and to create in thought and in material**

These motives are listed in the approximate order of their importance and greatest usefulness.

The super-salesman checks his sales presentation against these nine basic motives to make sure that it embraces an appeal through as many of them as possible. He knows that a sales presentation is more effective when based upon more than one motive.

No salesman has any right to try to sell anything to anyone unless he can present through his sales argument a logical motive for the purchaser to buy, and no super-salesman will try to do so. Super-salesmanship contemplates the rendering of useful service to the buyer. High-pressure methods do not come within the category of super-salesmanship, mainly for the reason that such methods presuppose the lack of a logical motive for buying. The very fact that high-pressure methods are employed is evidence that the person doing the selling has no logical motive to offer the prospective purchaser as to why he or she should buy.

High-pressure salesmen usually depend upon superlatives to take the place of motives for buying. This is a form of hi-jacking to which Master Salesmen never resort.

If your sales presentation plan does not emphasize one or more of the nine basic motives, it is weak and should be revised. Careful analysis of over 30,000 sales people disclosed the fact that the outstanding weaknesses of approximately 98 per cent of them were to be found among the following:

WEAKNESSES IN TECHNIQUE

1. **Failure to present a motive for buying**
2. **Lack of persistence in sales presentation and in closing**
3. **Failure to qualify prospective buyers**
4. **Failure to neutralize the minds of prospective buyers**
5. **Lack of imagination**
6. **Absence of enthusiasm**

These deficiencies are common among the majority of sales people in all fields of selling. Any one of these weaknesses is sufficient to destroy the chances of a sale.

You will observe that "failure to present motive for buying" heads the list of six most common weaknesses of sales people. Nothing but indifference or lack of knowledge of scientific selling could explain this weakness.

THE MAJOR WEAKNESSES
IN PERSONALITY AND HABITS OF SALESMEN

Success in selling is the result of positive qualities which one must possess and use. Failure in selling is the result of negative qualities which should be eliminated. Among the more outstanding negative qualities are the following:

1. ***The habit of procrastination.*** There is no substitute for
    prompt and persistent action.
2. ***One or more of the six basic fears.*** The man whose
    mind is filled with any form of fear cannot sell successfully.
    The six basic fears are:

    (a) The fear of poverty
    (b) The fear of criticism
    (c) The fear of ill health
    (d) The fear of loss of love of someone
    (e) The fear of old age
    (f) The fear of death

    To this list of basic fears should, perhaps, be added fear that
    the prospective buyer will bite the salesman.
3. ***Spending too much time making "calls" instead of
    sales.*** A "call" is not an interview. An interview is not a
    sale. Some who call themselves salesmen have not learned
    this truth.
4. ***Shifting responsibility to the sales manager.*** The sales
    manager is not supposed to go with the salesman to make
    calls. He has not enough hours or legs to do this. His business
    is to tell the salesman what to do, not to do it for him!
5. ***Perfection in creating alibis.*** Explanations do not
    explain. Orders do! Nothing else does! Don't forget that!
6. ***Spending too much time in hotel lobbies.*** A hotel
    lobby is a fine place to "park" but the salesman who parks
    there too long is bound to get walking papers sooner or later.
7. ***Buying "hard-luck" stories instead of selling
    merchandise.*** The "Business Recession" is a common
    topic of discussion, but don't let the purchasing agent use it
    to switch your mind from your own story.
8. ***Imbibing too freely "the night before."*** Parties are
    exciting, but they do not add to the following day's business.
9. ***Depending on the sales manager for "prospects."***
    Order-takers expect prospective buyers to be hog tied and
    held down until they arrive. Master Salesmen catch their

own prospects on the wing. This is one of the chief reasons why they are "master salesmen"

10. ***Waiting for business conditions to pick up.*** Business is always good with the robins, but they do not wait for someone to dig the worms out of the ground. Be at least as clever as a robin! Orders are not being slipped under the salesman's door this year.

11. ***Hearing the word "no."*** This word, to a real salesman is only a signal to begin fighting. If every buyer said "yes" salesmen would have no jobs, for they would not be needed.

12. ***Fearing competition.*** Henry Ford has plenty of competition, but he apparently does not fear it because he had the courage and ability to turn out an eight-cylinder car at an amazingly low price during a period in which many motor manufacturers were retrenching.

13. ***Devoting too much time to the "poultry" business.*** The only sort of chickens that lay eggs are the feathered variety, and they roost on farms, *not on Broadway or Main Street!*

14. ***Reading the stock market reports.*** Let the "suckers" bite at this bait. You may be smart enough to dodge the "hook" but think how the sales manager would feel if you won a fortune on the stock market and quit the house, as one out of every ten thousand who play the market do—*sometimes!*

15. ***Plain pessimism.*** The habit of expecting that the prospective buyer will give you the gate is likely to result in your getting it. Life has a queer way of trying to please. It usually gives that which is expected!

This is not a complete list of "Salesmen's Don'ts," but it is a fair sample. Perhaps some may interpret the list to be a little too personal and flippant. Others may see in it as a touch of sarcasm. Remember, as you read, that it was intended only for those who have corns on their toes. Others will not be offended. If you have any doubt as to whether or not you are suffering from any of these "Don'ts," pick up courage and check the list over with your sales manager, first assuring him with hands crossed on your heart, that you want him to be perfectly frank with you!

This list of "Don'ts" is not original with me. It was compiled from observation of more than 30,000 salesmen whom I have had the privilege of training, some of whom I have directed.

Need I suggest that not one of these "Don'ts" is an attribute of a pleasing personality?

*   *   *   *   *

"Successful people, in all callings, never stop acquiring knowledge related to their major purpose, business, or profession."
– Napoleon Hill

*   *   *   *   *

CHAPTER 5

Auto-Suggestion, Your First Step In Salesmanship

E very super-salesman knows that every sale is first made to the salesman, himself, and that the extent to which the salesman convinces himself in making this sale, measures perfectly the degree of conviction which can be introduced in the buyer's mind.

Because of the importance of self-selling, the subject of auto-suggestion assumes an important role in the teaching of salesmanship. This is the principle through which the salesman saturates his own mind with belief in the commodity or service offered for sale, as well as in his own *ability* to sell.

Auto-suggestion is self-suggestion. It is the principle through which one imparts to one's subconscious mind any idea, plan, concept, or belief. The sub-conscious mind is the "broadcasting station" which voluntarily "telegraphs" one's thoughts and beliefs (or disbeliefs) to others. The super-salesman knows he must "educate" his sub-conscious mind to broadcast belief in that which he offers for sale.

Repetition of a suggestion to one's sub-conscious mind is the most effective way of "educating" it to broadcast only such thoughts as will be beneficial. The sub-conscious mind will not be influenced by any suggestions made to it except those that are mixed with feelings or emotion. The head, or cold reasoning faculty, has no influence whatsoever on the sub-conscious mind. It responds only to the impulses of thought, which have been well mixed with feeling. The sub-conscious mind is influenced by the negatives as readily as by the positives. Super-salesman never overlook this fact! This is one reason they are super-salesman!

THE SEVEN MAJOR POSITIVE EMOTIONS

1. **The emotion of sex (Placed at the head of the list because it is the most powerful emotion)**
2. **The emotion of love**
3. **The emotion of hope**
4. **The emotion of faith**
5. **The emotion of enthusiasm**
6. **The emotion of optimism**
7. **The emotion of loyalty**

The world is controlled by the emotional faculty!

Most of our activities, from birth until death, are introduced by our "feelings." The salesman who appeals to his buyers through their emotions or "feelings" will make ten sales to one made by the salesman who appeals to his buyers through their reason alone. Buyers generally make purchases because of some motive that is closely associated with the emotions, as one may readily discern by studying the table of motives which prompt people to buy.

In the foregoing list of seven major positive emotions, the super-salesman will find nature's "elixir" which he must mix with the suggestions he plants in the sub-conscious mind if he expects to broadcast to his prospective customers through impulses which will influence them in his favor.

THE SEVEN MAJOR NEGATIVE EMOTIONS

1. **The emotion of anger (Quick and transitory)**
2. **The emotion of fear (Prominent and easily discernible)**
3. **The emotion of greed (Subtle and persistent)**
4. **The emotion of jealously (Impulsive and spasmodic)**
5. **The emotion of revenge (Subtle and quiet)**
6. **The emotion of hatred (Subtle and persistent)**
7. **The emotion of superstition (Subtle and slow)**

The presence of any one of these emotional impulses, in the conscious mind, is sufficient to discourage presence of all of the positive emotions. In extreme cases, the presence of a combination of these emotions, in the conscious mind, may lead to insanity.

Obviously, any suggestion planted in the sub-conscious mind while any one or more of these negative emotions is present, will carry with it a coloring of a negative nature. When the sub-conscious mind "broadcasts" any such suggestion, it will register a negative result in the minds of those who "pick up" the vibration.

Understand this principle and you will know why a super-salesman must first sell himself before trying to sell others. You will also know why the negative-minded salesman hears the "No" so often. Feelings, beliefs, and thoughts released by the salesman, through his sub-conscious mind, speak more loudly than words. Remember that people are motivated to buy, or not to buy, through their feelings. Remember also that much of what they believe to be, their own "feelings," consist, in reality, of thought impulses which they have unconsciously picked up from vibrations of thought released by the salesman.

The super-salesman neither permits his sub-conscious mind to "broadcast" negative thoughts nor gives expression to them through words, for the reason that he understands the "like attracts like" and negative suggestions attract negative action and negative decisions from prospective purchasers.

The salesman who "knocks" anything or anyone thereby destroys the advantage he might obtain through positive suggestion. The presence in the mind of even one of the negative emotions has a tendency to attract to it a flock of its relatives. Knowing this, the super-salesman takes care not to plant negative thoughts in the minds of his prospective purchasers.

Politics and politicians, as is well known to every reader, are in ill repute all over the country today. Analyze the brand of salesmanship used by politicians, and you may readily understand why they have lost confidence of their "buyers." It is customary for those who seek office to do so by attacking their competitors for office, instead of selling themselves to the voters on their own merit. No well-managed business would permit salesman to seek patronage by knocking competitors. Sales managers have enough common sense to know that sales made by belittling competitors or competitive merchandise are not really sales and that business obtained in this way is a liability in the long run.

Any political speech is, as a rule, a fine example of just this sort of salesmanship.

A wise philosopher once said, "Whom the Gods would destroy, they first make mad." Anger is a negative emotion. It makes a very poor salve when mixed with salesmanship, whether or not there be just cause for anger. Silence is far more effective than words inspired by and mixed with the emotion of anger.

Satire, sarcasm, and negative thoughts expressed by innuendo may give a salesman a reputation as a wise-cracker, but they will not aid him in selling his wares. Out and out statements of a negative nature are the equivalent of suicide selling.

The taxicab companies of New York City engaged in a price war some time ago. The public resented their tactics and registered its resentment through a loss to the business of over $750,000.00 in one year!

It used to be a popular pastime for automobile salesmen to endeavor to make sales by knocking competitive cars. More than a hundred automobile manufacturers were forced to the wall before they awoke to the fact that anything which hurts one man's business hurts all business in that line.

Life insurance men used to follow the practice of "twisting" (including the owner of a policy in a competitive company to give up that policy and purchase one in his company). Intelligent life insurance officials stopped the practice except in isolated cases. "Twisting," with most life insurance companies, is considered the equivalent of a discharge. The agent who does it will not be tolerated any longer than is required to find him out.

Negative statements in selling not only set up resentment in the minds of the prospective buyer, but they magnetize the salesman's own sub-conscious mind so that it throws off negative vibrations which are picked up by other people and acted upon to the detriment of the salesman.

*   *   *   *   *

"Never, in the history of the world, has there been such an abundant opportunity as there is now for the person who is willing to serve before trying to collect."

– Napoleon Hill

*   *   *   *   *

CHAPTER 6
The Master Mind

In selling, as in every walk of life, noteworthy achievement is predicated upon power.

> **Power is acquired through organized and intelligently directed knowledge. The Master Mind principle makes available unlimited sources of knowledge, because one may, through its application, avail one's self to the knowledge possessed by others, as well as all knowledge which has been accumulated and recorded.**

The term "Master Mind" means the coordination of two or more minds, working in perfect harmony, for a definite purpose."

There are two separate and distinct phases of this principle. One is economic in nature, the other psychic. Through aid of the economic phase, it is obvious that one may, through friendly alliance with other, avail one's self of their knowledge, experience, and cooperative efforts. The psychic (spiritual) phase leads in an entirely different direction from the economic phase. This portion of the Master Mind principle may be used to connect one's conscious, thinking mind with the higher forces of Infinite Intelligence. I regret that limited space makes it impracticable to describe here in detail the psychic phase of the Master Mind. (This principle has been fully covered in *The Law of Success* by this same author).

The economic phase. Let us keep in mind the fact that power is essential for successful achievement in every walk of life. Also, let us remember, power is organized and intelligently directed knowledge. These facts indicate clearly that power in great quantities can be accumulated only through coordinated efforts of a plurality of minds. No one individual, functioning independently, can ever possess great power, no matter how intelligent or well informed he may be, for the reason that power must be transmitted before it is effective; one individual is limited as to the amount of power he can transmit or apply.

The reader should gain a clear understanding of the two phases of the Master Mind principle at the outset of this chapter, even at the risk of dealing with principles which seem more abstract than concrete. The Master Mind principle is the basis of all great, enduring power. It must, therefore, be understood and applied by all who attain to mastery in any calling, in selling as well as in other vocations.

Henry Ford has organized one of the most efficient Master Mind groups known in the entire field of distribution. This group consists of his thousands of trained dealers who operate in practically every part of the world. Through the cooperative efforts of his dealer alliance, Mr. Ford can estimate, well in advance of the actual building of his cars, how many can be distributed. He knows where his market exists and the extent of that market, even before the raw materials for his cars have been assembled. His greatest asset is his Master Mind sales alliance. This is an indisputable fact. Mr. Ford owes his stupendous success to his understanding and application of the Master Mind principle.

Andrew Carnegie first brought to my attention the Master Mind principle. He attributed his huge fortune to his use of it. His Master Mind group consisted of about twenty men, his executive staff, whose combined technical knowledge and experience enabled him to make and market steel successfully. Mr. Carnegie informed me that he could have made his fortune in the grocery business or banking business or railroad business or in any business which rendered useful service to a large number of people just as easily as he made it in the steel business. By merely surrounding himself with men whose knowledge and temperament were suited to the pursuit of the business in which he might be engaged.

The Master Mind principle is the basis of every great fortune, even inherited fortunes were originally accumulated through the Master Mind principle.

Successful achievement is the result of power!

Power in great quantities can be accumulated only through application of the Master Mind principle. I have repeated this statement many times for the sake of emphasis because it contains the very essence of mastery and achievement.

*   *   *   *   *

"One way to avoid criticism is to do nothing!"
                                          – Napoleon Hill

*   *   *   *   *

CHAPTER 7
Your Improved Concentration

Only through the principle of *concentration* can the psychic phase of the Master Mind principle be reached and used. Concentration is the focusing of the attention, interest, and desire upon the attainment of a *definite* end. In view of these facts, it will be readily observed that concentration is essential for the effective use of the Master Mind principle, the two being inseparable when practical results are to be obtained through their use by two or more people.

Auto-suggestion (self-suggestion) is the principle through which the sub-conscious mind may be reached and influenced, concentration is the principle through which auto-suggestion must be applied, a fact which has been clearly illustrated in the chapter on that subject. We have termed it "the first step in salesmanship."

The Master Mind principle, the principle of Concentration and the principle of Auto-suggestion, constitute a triumvirate which must be used in reaching and influencing the sub-conscious mind.

The sub-conscious mind will not recognize nor be influenced by any suggestion given it unless that suggestion is mixed with one or more of the emotions mentioned in the chapter on auto-suggestion.

Thus, it will be seen that these three chapters on the Master Mind, Auto-suggestion, and Concentration constitute the very heart of Master Salesmanship. If you miss complete understanding and assimilation of these three chapters, this book will have lost for you much of its value.

In this chapter is described the method by which the principle of concentration may be applied effectively. Don't fail to make the most of it, for it is of supreme importance to you.

Concentration is defined as "the habit of planting in the mind a definite aim, object or purpose, and visualizing the same until ways and means for its realization have been created."

The principle of concentration, as it applies to and constitutes a part of mastery in selling embraces planting in one's conscious mind a definite chief aim, idea, plan, or purpose and the continuous focusing upon it of the conscious mind.

The principle of concentration is the medium by which procrastination is overcome. The same principle is the foundation upon which both self-confidence and self-confidence are predicted.

The Law of Habit. The principle of habit and the principle of concentration go hand in glove. Habit may grow out of concentration and concentration may grow out of habit.

The object of concentrating upon a definite aim is to train the mind until it forms the habit of focusing upon the object of that aim. By focusing upon one's definite aim through concentrated effort and attention, this habit comes to influence the sub-conscious mind so that it picks up the mental concept of that aim and translates it into its physical counterpart through the most practical and direct methods available.

Every human being makes use of the principle of concentration whether he realizes it or not. The person who permits his conscious mind to dwell upon the negative thoughts of fear, poverty, ill health, and intolerance, thereby applies the law of concentration and sooner or later the sub-conscious mind will pick up these suggestions and act upon them and translate them into their counterparts. .

INSTRUCTIONS FOR APPLYING CONCENTRATION

1. Master and apply the principles described in the chapter of *Auto-suggestion* by following the habit of giving orders to your sub-conscious mind, mixing your thoughts with one or more of the positive emotions and repeating your orders over and over. Keep up this procedure until you get satisfactory results, remembering that eternal vigilance is the price of mastery in this effort.

2. Empty your conscious mind of all other thoughts. After a little practice you will be able to focus your mind entirely upon any subject that you please. The act of focusing upon one subject and keeping your mind upon that one subject is concentration.

3. Hold your thoughts to the object of your concentration with a *burning desire* for the attainment of whatever object you have in mind. When concentrating upon your Definite Chief Aim, do so in perfect faith that you will realize the object of that aim.

4. When you find your conscious mind wandering, drive it back and focus it upon that subject again and again until you have developed such perfect self-control that you can keep out of your mind all other thoughts. *Mix emotions or "feeling" with your thoughts when concentrating; otherwise they will not be recognized by your sub-conscious mind.*

5. The principle of concentration may be best applied when one is in an environment of silence where there are no counter attractions or noises of any disturbing nature. The best time for concentrating is after one has retired at night, for then the number of distractions is minimized.

6. Your sub-conscious mind can best be reached and influenced when you concentrate in your conscious mind upon an idea, plan, or purpose in a spirit of *intense enthusiasm*, for the reason that enthusiasm arouses your faculty of creative imagination and puts it into action.

> **Any idea, plan, or purpose or definite aim which you persistently submit to your sub-conscious mind through the medium of concentration here described, brings to your aid the force of infinite intelligence until eventually practical plans of procedure will flash into your mind during your period of concentration.**

When you first start your practice of concentration, you may not experience the feeling that you are in communication with a superior intelligence, but in time if you develop the habit of regular concentration, you will be thoroughly cognizant of the fact that a superior intelligence is influencing you.

It is a well-known fact that the jack-of-all-trades never achieves success. Life is so very complicated and there are many ways of dissipating energy unprofitably that the habit of concentrated effort must be formed and adhered to by all who succeed.

Power is predicted upon organized energy. Energy can only be organized through the principle of concentration. It is a fact worthy of serious consideration that all men of outstanding success in all walks of life are men who concentrate the major portion of their thoughts and efforts upon some one definite purpose or chief aim.

By analyzing the principle of the Master Mind, you will observe that when two or more people ally themselves in a spirit of harmony for the purpose of achieving some definite object, that alliance functions through the principle of concentrated effort.

From my analysis of more than 25,000 men and women who were rated as failures, I observed that none of them followed the habit of focusing his mind upon a definite chief aim through the principle of concentration. The thirty major causes of failure may be either controlled or eliminated entirely through the principle of concentration, indicating the importance of this principle as a part of the working equipment of the successful salesman.

> **Nearly everyone has a definite chief aim at one time or another. Ninety-five percent of the people who have such aims, however, make no attempt to realize them, for the reason they have not learned the art of concentrating on their definite aims for sufficient length of time to fix in the sub-conscious mind the object of their aims. The majority of the people who adopt a definite aim, do so more in the nature of a wish than in the form of a definite, determined, well-defined intention.**

Merely permitting a definite aim to come into one's mind is in no way beneficial. Such an aim, to be of permanent value, must be fixed in the mind through the principle of concentration.

Concentration develops the power of persistence and enables one to master all forms of temporary defeat. The majority of people never learn the real difference between temporary defeat and permanent failure, for the reason that they are lacking in the persistence necessary to stage a comeback after they have experienced temporary defeat. Persistence is merely concentrated effort well mixed with determination and faith.

From these facts, you will readily understand that the principle of a Definite Chief Aim and the principle of Concentration are complementary. One can be applied successfully only with the aid of the other.

> **Every human being is ruled by the law of habit. Because this is true, the person who learns to build his habits to order practically controls the major cause of successful achievement. Concentration is the principle through which one may build one's habits to order. It has been correctly said that "we first make our habits and our habits then make us."**

We have habits of mind and habits of body. Both are subject to control and the medium of that control is concentration. The mind is just as susceptible to the influence of habit as is the physical body. Through concentration, we may force the mind to dwell upon any subject we desire until the mind falls into the habit of dwelling on that subject. It then follows the habit automatically.

There is no point of compromise between a man and his habits. Either he controls his habits or his habits control him. The successful man, understanding this truth, forces himself to build the sort of habits by which he is willing to be controlled.

Habits are formed step by step through our every thought and deed.

Center your thoughts upon a Definite Aim, through concentration, and very soon your sub-conscious mind will pick up a clear picture of that aim and aid you in translating it into it's physical counterpart.

All thought has a tendency to externalize itself. This is a truth well known to every psychologist, as it was known to him who wrote, "Whatever a man soweth, that shall he also reap."

> **Your financial condition is not the result of chance or accident. It reflects perfectly the nature of your dominating thoughts, desires, and aims. In analyses of men who have accumulated huge fortunes I studied particularly the source of those fortunes and in every case discovered that they represented the consummation of the state of mind of those who had accumulated them.**

The man who understands the possibilities of concentration, need rarely know the word "impossible."

Throughout this book I have repeatedly made reference to the power of infinite intelligence. If such a power can be influenced to inject itself into man's affairs and made to help man achieve the object of his aims and purposes, I feel certain that this stupendous result can be attained only through the principle of concentration.

I owe eternal allegiance to Infinite Intelligence. No church nor creed would quarrel with such an attitude. This statement is made for the sole purpose of enabling every reader to become more familiar with a great universal law that is capable of being harnessed and induced to separate man from all of his causes of doubt, worry, and fear.

I am a firm believer in the power of prayer. Let me explain, however, what I mean by the term "prayer." To me a prayer is any fixed or definite aim which is founded upon faith in the realization of that purpose or aim. Concentration without faith appears to bring no results. Concentration with faith appears to achieve results, which border on the miraculous.

The process of mixing faith with a definite chief aim is one which is indeed difficult to describe and more difficult still to apply. Faith can only be induced through concentration upon

the object of one's hopes, aims, and purposes.

A little while before his death, I had the privilege of visiting with the late F. W. Woolworth. In these words did he describe the method through which he built what was at the time the tallest building in the world:

"I had an architect draw up a set of plans. Every day for more than six months I went into my private office, shut the door and looked over these plans for more than half and hour. Each time I looked at them the actual physical building seemed nearer a reality. Finally the day came when the exact method by which I financed the Woolworth Building flashed into my mind and I knew instantly that the building was a reality. From that point on, I had no difficulty whatsoever."

The Woolworth Building became a reality because F. W. Woolworth concentrated upon that building *until concentrated thought externalized itself in physical reality.*

Writing in *The Christian Science Monitor*, Mr. Willis J. Abbot recently said:

"I was in the original Menlo Park laboratory of Edison, which Henry Ford, with pious reverence for the great inventor had erected at Dearborn, Michigan. All of the earlier tools of Edison's craft are there—the first electric incandescent light—it had a life of eight hours; the first phonograph, in which a needle played over a tin-foil, recorded and emitted a squeaky imitation of the human voice. Thousands of bottles of chemicals lined the walls. 'Mr. Edison had to have every known chemical where he could put his hand on it,' said the custodian, who had worked with him half a century ago.

But to me, more interesting than the material relics was a picture the custodian drew for me, little thinking how impressive it was. 'Often Mr. Ford comes in here,' said he. 'He pulls up that chair and just sits and thinks. Sometimes he'll sit almost an hour and then go out without a word to anyone.'

"What are the thoughts of the giant of industrial organization as he sits thus surrounded by the relics of the earlier triumphs of Edison's wizardry. 'Thinking,' he once said, 'is the hardest work that any man can do.' Perhaps he found it easier to think out his problems in an environment that had witnessed the solution of so many. At any rate, the spectacle of Henry Ford thus plunged in mediation amidst the evidences of Edison's struggles and victories is one to challenge thought."

It is difficult for anyone to say which of the principles described in this book is the most important, but I always feel when I approach the subject of Concentration that I am dealing with the keystone to the arch of the whole subject.

* * * * *

"Your employer does not control the sort of service you render. You control that, and it is the thing that makes or breaks you."

– Napoleon Hill

* * * * *

CHAPTER 8
Initiative And Leadership

Initiative means the doing of things without being told to do them. It means the selection of a Definite Aim and the building of plans for the achievement of that aim.

Its most profitable application is in the selection of a Master Mind group. If you use judgement in selection of this group, your Master Mind alliance will give you the power of real leadership.

THE MAJOR ATTRIBUTES OF INITIATIVE AND LEADERSHIP

In applying initiative and leadership, certain definite steps are essential. The following are the most important of these steps:

1. Know *definitely* what you want.
2. Build a practical plan or plans for the achievement of that which you want, making use of the counsel and advice of your Master Mind group.
3. Surround yourself with an organization made up of men who have the knowledge and experience essential for carrying out your Definite Aim.
4. Have sufficient faith in yourself and in your plans to see your aim a finished reality even before you begin to carry out your plans.
5. Do not become discouraged no matter with what obstacles you may meet. If one plan fails to work substitute other plans until you have found the one that will work.

6. Do no guessing but get the facts as the basis for all of your plans.

7. Do not be influenced by others to abandon your plans or your aim.

8. Have no set hours of labor. The leader must devote to his task whatever hours are necessary for success.

9. Concentrate upon one thing at a time as you cannot dissipate thought and energy and still be efficient.

10. Whenever possible relegate to others the responsibility of details, but have a system for checking your subordinates to see that these details are accurately attended to. Hold yourself accountable at all times for carrying out all of your plans, bearing in mind that if subordinates fail, it is you yourself who have failed.

Persistence is the keynote to success for all great leaders. If you are going to become discouraged at the first signs of opposition or adversity, you will never become a great leader. Leadership means the capacity to assume great responsibility. If you lack the quality of persistence, you must have associated with you in your Master Mind group some person or persons who have this quality. An efficient leader never permits himself to be loaded down with small details. One of the outstanding qualities of a leader is the ability to so organize his plans that he is free at all times to place the weight of his personal effort wherever it is most needed. I have met and interviewed, many times, many of the most able industrial leaders of America. Not one of these ever seemed to be rushed with work, for the reason that in every case the responsibility of details had been relegated to others.

The man who boasts of the habit of inspecting personally all the details of his business is either not an able leader or he is at the head of a very small business. The sentence "I haven't had time" is said to be the most dangerous sentence in the English language. Any man who makes such an admission confesses his lack of ability as a leader. The real leader has time for everything necessary to his successful leadership. The stock alibi of more than ninety percent of the world's failures, to justify them in not having selected a Definite Chief Aim in life, is "I just haven't had time to get around to it." An efficient leader is not necessarily the person who appears to be the busiest, but he is the person who can so organize his plans that he can efficiently direct and keep large numbers of other people busy. The man who can "get things done" is much more profitable to a business house than the man who actually does the work.

The efficient leader is also an efficient salesman. He gets people to do things because they wish to do them *for him*. The efficient leader has a pleasing personality. He is optimistic and enthusiastic and he knows how to transmit his enthusiasm and his optimism to his followers. An efficient leader is courageous. No man wishes to follow a leader who is lacking in courage, and in fact, will not do so. The efficient leader has a keen sense of justice and deals with his followers fairly and justly. An efficient leader assumes full responsibility for the acts of his subordinates. If they make mistakes, he assumes that it is he that has really made the mistake because it was he who chose the subordinates. The efficient leader understands the rules of pedagogy and is in reality an able *teacher. An efficient leader reaches decisions quickly and changes them slowly.*

There are circumstances, of course, which call for slow deliberation and the examination of facts before an intelligent decision can be reached. However, after all the available facts have been gathered and organized, there is no excuse for delaying decision, and the person who practices the habit of delay cannot become an effective leader unless he masters this shortcoming. For more than a hundred years there had been "talk" about the building of the Panama Canal, but the actual work of building the Canal never got much beyond the "talk" stage until the late Theodore Roosevelt became President of the United States. With the firmness of decision which was the very warp and woof of his achievements and the real basis of his reputation as a leader, Roosevelt took the initiative, had a bill framed for Congress to pass, providing for the appropriation, organized his Master Mind group of engineers, went to work with a spirit of self-confidence and lo, the much talked of Panama Canal became a splendid reality.

We have had more learned men than Theodore Roosevelt in the White House, but we have had few, if any, greater leaders than he. Leaders are men of action!

General Grant said, "We will fight it out on this line if it takes all summer," and despite his many other deficiencies, he stood by that decision and won.

When asked by one of his sailors what he would do if they saw no signs of land by the following day, Columbus replied, "If we see no land tomorrow, we will sail on and on." He, too, had a Definite Chief Aim and a plan for its attainment, and he too, had reached a decision not to quit or turn back until success had crowned his efforts. Columbus was a man with a great ability as a leader.

Napoleon, when surprised by the enemy, having discovered that there was a deep camouflaged ditch just ahead of the line of march, gave orders for his cavalry to charge the ditch. He waited until the dead bodies of men and horses filled the ditch, then marched his troops across and whipped the enemy. That required courage and quick decision; moreover, it required instantaneous decision. One minute of faltering or hesitation and he would have been flanked by the enemy and captured. He did the unexpected or "impossible." His capacity to act quickly *without waiting to be told by others what to do* was the quality which marked him as a great leader.

The first step essential to the development of Initiative and Leadership, is that of forming the habit of prompt and *firm* decision. The great leader must have a tremendous amount of capacity for quick and prompt decision. The man who hesitates between vague notions of what he wants to do or should do, generally ends by doing nothing.

This is an age where when initiative and leadership are in demand in practically every calling. Never in the history of the world have these qualities meant as much as they do today for the reason that millions of people throughout the world are in an unsettled, undecided state of mind. In America the doors are wide open to men who have the qualities of initiative and leadership in statesmanship, religion, industry, finance, transportation, merchandising, education, and in a score of other lines of endeavor. At the present time there are few outstanding men in any of these great fields.

There is a mistaken notion in the world to the effect that a man is paid for what he knows. This is only partly true, and like all other half-truths, it does more damage than an out and out falsehood. The truth is: a man is paid, not merely for that which he knows, but more particularly for *what he does with what he knows, or that which he can get others to do.*

Not long ago the author received a letter from a man who said, "I have a splendid education and I could be a great success if someone would only show me what to do or how to do it."

> **Successful men never wait for others to show them what to do or how to do it. They take the initiative themselves, appoint themselves to leadership, enlist the necessary assistance and capital and forge ahead despite all opposition. Self-confidence is one of the essentials for success in leadership. One of the natural tendencies of human nature is that of willingness to follow the man with great self-confidence. No one wishes to follow a man who does not seem to be sure of himself. It was said of Napoleon that his soldiers would willingly follow him to their death because of his example of courage and self-confidence.**

A real leader is always persistent and never accepts temporary defeat as failure. The leader who changes his mind often soon loses the confidence of his followers. When a leader changes his mind often he thereby puts his followers on notice that he is not sure of himself, and if he isn't sure of himself, how may he expect his followers to be sure of him.

The real leader shows no partiality among his followers. If he has friends or relatives in his organization, he treats them exactly as he does the rest of the staff.

A real leader not only has self-reliance and courage himself, but he imparts these qualities to his subordinates. When Mr. Cyrus H.K. Curtis placed a man in charge of one of his publications, he said to that man, "I am turning this property over to you to be managed and run just exactly as if you had the legal title to it. Make your own decisions, select your own help, create your own policy, lay out your own plans and then accept the entire responsibility for its success. All I wish to see is a satisfactory balance sheet at the end of the year."

Mr. Curtis was one of the most successful publishers in the world. He was successful because he himself was a great leader and his leadership was based primarily upon his understanding of the principle of relegating responsibility to others. He would not permit his subordinates to shift any responsibility back to him. In this way he created efficient leaders.

The President of the United States would get nowhere if he undertook to instruct all of his associates how to plan and conduct their campaigns. He places on their shoulders the responsibility of planning and carrying out the plans. The able business leader must do this. A man always does his best work when he feels that he is acting upon his own initiative and knows he must assume full responsibility for his actions.

There can be no real leadership in any calling without assumption of responsibility. We all want to be leaders in one way or another. Most of us would like to have the authority and the pay that belongs to the man who tells other people what to do, but few of us wish to accept the responsibility that goes with that authority. A real leader has not set hours of labor for the reason that it is his business to carry out his plans no matter how many hours he may be called upon to devote to the task.

The real leader makes due allowance for the ordinary weaknesses of his subordinates and lays his plans so he will be protected against these weaknesses. The real leader does not merely surround himself a number of subordinates selected at random. He selects with care the right man for the special job, later shifting and changing men from one job to another whenever and wherever he finds he has made a mistake. The real leader has a keen imagination and he induces action on the part of his followers by appeal to their imaginations. He does not rely upon his authority or power over his men, nor does he try to instill fear in their hearts. The real leader relies mainly upon his ability to sell his followers on doing what is most advantageous to him, through presenting the advantages to them. He uses *persuasion*, not power. ***There are two types of leaders in the world. One resorts to power and controls his followers through fear; the other resorts to persuasion and controls his followers through able salesmanship. Men of the latter type are Master Salesmen, regardless of their calling.***

In warfare, leadership based upon power and authority and fear may be essential, but in business that form of leadership is despicable. The successful leader in business and industry is a man who induces people to do things because it is to their advantage to do them and not merely because he happens to be in power.

The Master Salesman is essentially a leader. He induces people to cooperate with him in a spirit of harmony by planting in their minds adequate motives. He uses persuasion instead of coercion, therefore, his leadership endures. The Master Salesman reaches his followers and influences them favorably through their emotions as well as their reason.

All great leaders are Master Salesmen!

And all Master Salesmen are great leaders. They understand the art of persuasion; they understand how to set up in the minds of their followers motives which will induce favorable, willing cooperation.

Master Salesmen can sell anything they choose to sell because they have sufficient initiative to create markets. Moreover, they can sell one commodity, idea, plan, form of service, or motive as easily as any other.

Great leaders and Master Salesmen use the same philosophy. They sell their followers or patrons whatever they choose to sell by establishing a relationship of confidence.

* * * * *

"One of the greatest leaders who ever lived stated the secret of his leadership in six words, as follows: "Kindness is more powerful than compulsion."

– Napoleon Hill

* * * * *

CHAPTER 9
Archival And Current Photos

Napoleon Hill Country – Above is Powell Valley, near Stone Gap, in Wise County. This is a favorite area for tourists visiting Virginia. **"Young Nap"** often walked alone in this valley and dreamed of his future. **Napoleon Hill** drew inspiration from the natural scenic beauty of Wise County. The scenic walk and overlook (shown in photo) were built since the days of **Napoleon Hill's** youth. The above photograph of this scene, by award-winning Wise County photographer, **Tim Cox**, has been used in state tourism promotion and internationally.

Coal mines, such as the above operation in Wise County, Virginia, were essentially the only form of employment available for young men during the first 20 years of **Napoleon Hill's** life (1883-1903) in this depressed area.

The Wise County, Virginia, mine pictured above was one of the "finest coal mines" in **"Napoleon Hill** Country during it's time. This was then a state-of-the-art facility. **Napoleon Hill** became a Mine Manager while still a teenager.

"Farm or work in the mines!" This was the only career choice during **Napoleon Hill's** youth. The mine shown here looks orderly and safe but actual working conditions were brutal and often very dangerous. Copyrighted © 2005 Tim Cox. Used with permission.

International acclaimed photographer **Tim Cox** has captured the beauty of Napoleon Hill Country and has coal mine scenes of an earlier era. His photographic art is available from **Tim Cox Photo/Graphics**, 604 Nelson Avenue, N.E., Wise, VA 24293. Phone 276-579-7277.

David K. "Straight Shooter" Straight (above) founded **Eagle's Nest Homes**, enabling people in 17-countries to purchase "more house for less money," plus he created one of America's most successful business opportunities, all by following **Napoleon Hill's** methods.

The one room **Laurel Grove School** where **Napoleon Hill** began his education. This building was located near the Pound River in Wise, Virginia.

In 1952 **Napoleon Hill** wrote *Think And Grow Rich*. This book became one of the best-selling books of all time. Today his work remains in print in over twenty countries. **Hill** used a manual **L. C. Smith** typewriter (shown in photo) to type the original manuscript for *Think and Grow Rich*. To date **Hill's** books have sold over 62-million copies.

Don M. Green, Executive Director of **The Napoleon Hill Foundation** is shown above with **Virginia State Historical Marker KA-14** which recognizes the area where **Napoleon Hill** was born on October 26, 1883.

Napoleon Hill (October 26, 1883 – November 8, 1970) wrote the world's all-time best-selling self-help book *Think And Grow Rich*. Two of his other books also became international best-sellers, *The Law Of Success* and *How To Sell Your Way Through Life*. This photo of **Napoleon Hill** seated in his favorite chair was for many years the official **Napoleon Hill** press photo.

Napoleon Hill wrote many famous books. Best known among his titles is the classic. *Think And Grow Rich*. Among **Napoleon Hill's** other best-sellers are *How To Sell Your Way Through Life*, *Law Of Success*, *How To Raise Your Own Salary* (shown above in 1953), and *The Master Key To Riches*, plus other titles.

Fred R. Kissling, CLU, MSPA, AEP, RFC, built the largest independent financial publishing company in the USA by following the methods advocated by **Napoleon Hill**. **Kissling** is also a highly successful insurance representative and owner of champion racehorses. He is shown above with Spanish Glitter, winner of over half a million dollars.

Copyrighted © 2005 *Financial Services Advisor* Magazine. Used with permission.

W. Clement Stone, insurance tycoon and philanthropist, used **Napoleon Hill's** techniques to become one of the wealthiest men in the world. **Napoleon Hill** and **W. Clement Stone** co-authored *Success Through A Positive Mental Attitude*.

Copyrighted © 2005 The Napoleon Hill Foundation. Used with permission.

Michael S. Kindberg, of the media advocacy and image-building agency Intergroup II/ Atlanta, Inc., that serves financial professionals, is shown with the famous *Stay The Course* poster. This 18" x 24" poster is available for $18.85 from **The Napoleon Hill World Learning Center**, Purdue University Calumet, 2300 173rd Street, Hammond, Indiana 46323.

Poster Copyright © 2001 The Napoleon Hill Foundation. Photo Copyrighted © 2005 *Leaders* Magazine. Used with permission.

Jan Cooper, Ph.D., is a successful American artist, top-selling author, professional speaker, university professor, and television personality. **Dr. Cooper** is host of the popular nationally-syndicated program ***Let God Make Your Life A Masterpiece***. **Dr. Cooper's** column ranks as the "best read" section of ***Mentors*** Magazine. **Dr. Cooper** confesses, "Possibly more than anyone, I owe a huge debt to **Napoleon Hill**. In my life and work I have applied **Napoleon Hill's** teachings. This has been the nucleus for all of my achievements."

Copyright © 2005 Mentors Magazine. Used with permission.

J. T. 'Dock' Houk, JD, Ph.D., CPhD., is CEO of the **National Heritage Foundation**. **The National Heritage Foundation** 'houses' more foundations than any other organization in the world. According to *Financial Services Advisor* Magazine: "**Houk** is America's most successful and most respected expert on foundations and their management."
J. T. 'Dock' Houk says, "We have always followed the teachings of **Napoleon Hill**, especially in the areas of ethics and accountability."

Copyrighted © 2005 National Heritage Foundation. Used with permission.

Rev. Dr. John Clements, the popular **BBC-TV** personality, and author of *Make Your Walls Tumble*, travels across England and Europe speaking in small unknown churches and large world-famous cathedrals. **Clements** is one of Britain's leading authorities on the works of **Napoleon Hill**.

Don M. Green (left) Executive Director of the **Napoleon Hill Foundation**, is shown above with **Forrest Wallace Cato**, editor of *Financial Services Advisor* magazine.

Today **Napoleon Hill** continues to be featured on magazine covers around the world. Above is a recent cover of ***The Inspirator International***, the Pacific-Rim's largest circulation English language magazine serving self-help, sales, and personal motivation.

Photo of Napoleon Hill Copyright © 2005 The Napoleon Hill Foundation.
Photo of *The Inspirator International* magazine cover Copyrighted © 2005 *The Inspirator International*.
Used with permission.

Charlie "Tremendous" Jones, author of *Life is Tremendous*, holds **Forrest Wallace Cato**, author of *What It Takes To Make You GREAT*, in a "headlock" during a light moment at an event honoring **Napoleon Hill**.

Photo Copyright © 2005 *The Inspirator International* Magazine. Used with permission.

Mark E. Matson, RFC, is, according to *Probe*, "Both famous and respected as **America's Abundance Coach**." He is possibly the most successful speaker and sales trainer working in the financial services industry today. According to *Leaders* Magazine, "**Matson** has been responsible for more highly successful financial planners than any other person or source." **Mark Matson** manages almost a billion dollars for clients from coast-to-coast. *Financial Services Advisor* Magazine reports, "Matson ranks among the top national performer in terms of outstanding results for clients." This handsome financial super-star frequently acknowledges the proven wisdom of **Napoleon Hill**. Mark says, "**Joe Matson**, my successful father, often quotes **Napoleon Hill** at family gatherings and business meetings. When I was a teenager my father gave me **Napoleon Hill's** books. During my important work for clients, every day I apply **Napoleon Hill's** success methods and techniques."

CHAPTER 10

"Qualifying" Your Prospective Buyer

In the actual process of selling, the first step is to qualify your prospective buyer. That is, the salesman should ascertain tactfully from the prospective buyer, and from other sources if possible, the following information which he will need in presenting his sales plan to the best advantage:

1. How much money is the prospective purchaser prepared to spend and how much should he be asked to spend?
2. Are conditions, including the prospective buyer's state of mind, favorable for closing the sale? If not, when are they likely to be?
3. Will the prospective buyer act for himself or must some lawyer, banker, wife, husband, relative, counselor, or other person be consulted before a decision can be reached? If so, who is the person to be consulted and for what specific purpose?
4. If the prospective buyer must consult another person before making a decision, will he permit the salesman to be present at the consultation? *This is highly important.* No salesman can afford for a third person to sit in judgement upon him and his wares without being present to present his own case.
5. Does the prospective buyer like to do most of the talking? If so, be sure to give him the opportunity. Every word a prospective buyer speaks will serve as a cue to what is in his mind. If the prospective buyer is not inclined to talk freely, induce him

to do so by asking leading questions which will bring out the desired information.

While qualifying the prospective buyer, the salesman will find it easy to ascertain just what "alibi" and what objections are likely to be offered when the closing point has been reached. The following are some of the most commonly-used alibis, to which practically all prospective buyers resort:

(a) The prospective buyer will claim he does not have the money. The Master Salesman always takes this one with more than the proverbial grain of salt. If the salesman has accurately qualified his prospective buyer, he knows his financial status and can, therefore, tactfully meet this objection.

(b) The prospective buyer, if he is a man, may tell the salesman that he does not wish to decide until he talks the matter over with his wife, banker, or lawyer. If he hides behind his wife's skirts, the Master Salesman will tactfully invite him to permit him (the salesman) to talk to the two of them together. At this interview the Master Salesman will analyze the wife and ascertain whether she is the real boss or a mere subterfuge for her husband. If she is the boss, he will direct his sales efforts mainly to her.

(c) The prospective buyer may claim he does not wish to reach a decision until he has had time to "think the matter over." That is an old one! The Master Salesman knows about how much "thinking" the majority of people do about anything. However, he will use tact in such cases, and will suggest ways and means by which he can assist his prospective buyer at his task of thinking. The Master Salesman permits his prospective buyers to believe they are doing their own thinking, but he takes care to see that they think with ideas and facts that he supplies.

All of this process of qualifying the prospective buyer must precede the attempt to close the sale. Practically every sale that is lost after the sales presentation has been made occurs for one of two reasons, mainly:

FIRST: Either the salesman has not properly "neutralized" the mind of his prospective buyer before making his sales presentation.

or

SECOND: He has failed to qualify accurately the prospective buyer before trying to close the sale.

The Master Salesman never tries to close a sale until he is absolutely sure that he has painted in the prospective buyer's mind a picture of which has created a strong desire for his wares. The prospective buyer must be able to buy. This is a point on which no guessing should be done. It is the Master Salesman's business to *know*, and if he does not know, he is not a Master Salesman!

Trying to sell a Packard automobile to a man who has only a Ford income and an Austin bank account is a wasted effort. Accurate qualification prevents such waste.

The first thing a Master Salesman asks a prospective purchaser of life insurance is "How much insurance do you now carry, and what sort of policies do you have?" Armed with this information, which is easily acquired for the asking, and knowing the prospective buyer's approximate financial status, the life insurance salesman knows what policy to offer his client.

THE QUESTION METHOD
OF QUALIFYING PROSPECTIVE BUYERS

Master Salesmen take the precaution of propounding an adequate supply of stock questions with which they acquire from their prospective purchasers such information as they need to qualify them accurately. Most men will answer any reasonable questions that are asked of them. Care and thought in the preparation and asking of these questions will enable the salesman to arm himself with all the information he needs to close a sale. Moreover, the information will be authentic and reliable because the prospect will supply it.

LET YOUR PROSPECT TALK FREELY

When police officials arrest a man who is suspected of having committed a crime, they proceed, immediately, to induce the suspect to talk! Every word he utters, as well as his refusal to talk on certain points, places in the hands of the investigators facts from which they can easily make important deductions.

Until the point of actual presentation of the sales plan has been reached every Master Salesman is, in reality, an investigator. It is his business to get the facts, and the best method for getting them is to induce the prospective buyer to talk! Some who call themselves salesmen spoil their chances of making sales by opening their mouths and closing their eyes and ears. The most successful salesmen manage an interview in such a tactful fashion that the prospective buyer believes *he* is managing it. When the sale has been closed, the buyer believes he has made a purchase rather than being sold anything.

QUALIFYING YOUR PROSPECTIVE BUYER

Master Salesmen make it a part of their technique to contact prospective buyers in advance of the time when any selling effort is made, for the purpose of qualifying them in an unobtrusive manner. One of the most successful life insurance salesmen in America specializes in the sale of life insurance policies to men with whom he plays golf. He takes great care, however, never to refer to his profession even briefly on the golf course. Moreover, he never tries to talk life insurance to his prospective buyers until after he has played golf with them at least three times, and even then he leads up to the subject through a series of cleverly prepared, tactful questions through which he induces his prospective buyers to ask him about life insurance. He calls himself a "Life Insurance Counselor." It is his business, he tells prospective buyers, to go over their life insurance policies with them for the purpose of ascertaining whether or nor they have the best form of insurance, the right amount, etc. Naturally, he chooses prospective buyers of insurance who carry large amounts of insurance and who, therefore, have many policies already in force. He has made hundreds of sales without asking his prospective buyers to take additional insurance, merely by analyzing their life insurance schedules in such a tactful way as to plant in their minds the though that they need additional insurance of one sort or another.

Confidence is the condition of major importance which must be created by the Master Salesman in the minds of his prospective buyers. If he qualifies his prospective buyers accurately, he builds this confidence while doing so. No sale of note can be made without this element of confidence. Master Salesmen often "stalk" their prospective buyers for months while establishing confidence, meanwhile refraining from any attempt to make sales.

Methods of Qualifying

The skilled detective often "plants" stool-pigeons where they can contact those who are suspected of crimes, for the purpose of gaining information about the suspect. Here again the Master Salesman follows tactics similar to those used by criminologist, but the Master Salesman acts as his own "stool-pigeon" and gets his information first handed. The nature of his work makes stealth in acquiring information unnecessary.

Sometimes, however, Master Salesman use skilled investigators. (They do not consider them to be "stool-pigeons.") These men are used for the purpose of gathering information about prospective buyers which the salesman themselves cannot acquire in person. This practice is common among salesmen who sell to public officials where the personal habits of those who are empowered to do the buying is believed to be questionable. It is the Master Salesman's business, among other things, to know all about his prospective buyer. He must get the facts.

Lobbyists, whose number in Washington is legion, often serve those who employ them, more in the capacity of investigators than they do as salesmen. If they find anything in the private habits of a Senator or a Congressman that will not bear the spotlight of publicity, the discovery becomes valuable to their employers. The same tactics are employed with

The law of compensation isn't always swift, but it is as certain as the setting of the sun.

reference to other Government officials whose cooperation sometimes is sought in the basis of coercion rather than persuasion

This form of qualification is most reprehensible! Moreover, it is accompanied by great hazards to the one who uses it. This method of securing information is mentioned, not with the object of recommending it, but for the purpose of showing how important it is for men who seek to "persuade" others, to have facts upon to which plan their sales presentation.

The salesman who is too indifferent or too lazy to supply himself with sufficient facts to enable him to qualify his prospective buyers deserves to fail, and he usually does.

Any man is nine-tenths beaten when his adversary gains possession of the motives by which he is most easily actuated, provided always that his adversary has the intelligence to use the information effectively. Master Salesmen possess this intelligence. Moreover, they become Master Salesmen largely because of their ability to gather facts and to qualify accurately their prospective buyers.

When police officials are called in to solve a murder mystery in which the motive for the murder is unknown, the first question they ask is, "Where is the woman in the case?" Or they may seek to determine whether robbery was a motive. Unless the motive for the crime has been established, it is often difficult to apprehend the criminal, and to convict him after he has been apprehended. These are facts from which the Master Salesman may profit. Find out the prospective buyer's major motives and his major weaknesses, and he is as good as in your bag before you begin.

*   *   *   *   *

> **"An educated person is not necessarily the one who has the knowledge, but the one who knows where to get the knowledge when needed!"**
> **– Napoleon Hill**

*   *   *   *   *

CHAPTER 11

Neutralizing Your Prospective Buyer's Mind

After the prospective buyer has been qualified or during the qualification process before a sale can be made, his mind must be emptied of prejudice, bias, resentment, and all other conditions unfavorable to the salesman. The prospective buyer's mind must be cultivated and prepared before the seed of desire can be successfully planted in it. A neutral or favorable mind of a prospective buyer should contemplate:

(a) **Confidence:** The buyer must have confidence in the salesman and in his wares.

(b) **Interest:** The buyer must be reached through an appeal to his imagination and interest, aroused in the commodity offered for sale.

(c) **Motive:** The buyer must have a logical motive for buying. The building of this motive is the salesman's most important task.

No prospective buyer's mind has been neutralized and made favorable until these three conditions exist in his mind. The salesman's first duty is to create confidence in the mind of his prospective buyer. Obviously, this cannot be done by arousing any of the negative emotions. It can only be done by careful analysis of:

1. The buyer
2. The buyer's business or calling

3. The obstacles which may face the buyer in the successful conduct of his business

Nothing builds confidence more quickly than a keen, a genuine interest in the buyer's business problems.

The salesman's second duty in preparing the mind of his prospect to receive favorably the seed of desire for his wares, is to arouse interest in those wares in the mind of the prospect. This may require the application of one or all of the "Qualities which a Master Salesman Must Possess," described in a preceding chapter. To arouse interest in his wares, the salesman will at least find it necessary to use imagination., faith, enthusiasm, and knowledge of his merchandise, persistence, and showmanship. A neutral mind will be of no advantage to the salesman who lacks the ability to plant in that mind the seed of desire for his merchandise. That seed cannot be planted without interest upon the part of the prospective buyer.

The salesman's third duty is to create an appropriate motive to induce the prospective buyer to purchase his wares. This will necessitate his having full and complete knowledge of the prospective buyer and his business or calling.

Failure to neutralize the mind of the prospective buyer is one of the five major weaknesses of the majority of unsuccessful salesmen. There can be no fixed rule to be followed in neutralizing the minds of prospective buyers, as each individual case offers conditions peculiar unto itself, and each case must be handled on its own merits. The salesman with imagination will not be slow to recognize the most appropriate methods of approach in neutralizing the minds of his prospective buyers. Some of the methods which have been used successfully for sales preparation or neutralization are as follows:

(a) **Social contacts through clubs.** It has been said that more business is done on the golf courses of America than is done in business offices. Certainly every super-salesman knows the value of club contacts.

(b) **Church affiliations.** Here one may make acquaintances without the usual formalities, under circumstances which tend to establish confidence.

(c) ***Lodge and union affiliations.*** In many lines of selling the salesman will find it highly helpful to establish contacts through lodges and trade unions, where men naturally let down the bars of formality.

(d) ***Personal courtesies.*** Dinner engagements offer favorable opportunity to break down the resistance of formalities and to establish confidence, a condition precedent to neutrality of mind.

(e) ***Personal service.*** Under some conditions salesmen are in a position to render valuable service and to supply helpful information to those with whom they intend to do business subsequently.

(f) ***Mutual interest in hobbies.*** Nearly every man has a hobby or some form of interest outside of his business or calling. When discussing or pursuing his hobby, one is always inclined to step out from the defense behind which he hides in the course of his business routine.

> **Having neutralized the mind of the buyer and having established confidence, the next step in making a sale is to crystallize that confidence into interest in the salesman's wares. Here the salesman must build his entire sales presentation around a central motive which is appropriate and best suited to the business and financial status of his prospective buyer. The three subjects of confidence, interest, and motive having been attended to, the salesman has reached the point at which the sale may be closed.**

SALESMANSHIP RESEMBLES A STAGE PLAY

Scientific salesmanship involves principles similar to those upon which a successful stage play is based. The psychology of selling an individual is closely akin to that which is used by actors in selling an audience. The stage play that succeeds must have the advantage of a strong opening act and a smashing climax, or closing act. If a play does not have these, it will be a flop.

ACT I   Must grip the attention and arouse the interest of the audience.

ACT II   Must develop plot or presentation. Though this be weak, it may yet go over, providing the first act has been strong. The audience (or buyers) will be charitable, providing they gained sufficient confidence from the first act to arouse expectation of a strong climax.

ACT III   Must realize the objective. This must be a knockout regardless of the first two acts or the play will be a flop. The third, or last act is where the sale is closed or lost.

The approach in selling must be strong enough to establish confidence and arouse interest in the salesman and his wares. If he falls down in this first act, he will experience difficulty, if not impossibility, in making a sale. The sales presentation may be weak at many places "in the middle" without fatality to the sale, providing the opening and the close are strong and impelling. The art of scientific salesmanship may be described as a Three Act Drama consisting of:

ACT I   *Interest* (This must be created by neutralizing the mind of the prospective buyer and establishing confidence.)

ACT II   *Desire* (Desire must be developed through the proper presentation of motive.)

ACT III   *Action* (Action or the close can be induced only by the proper presentation of the two preceding acts.)

It is hardly necessary to suggest that to the director (salesman) who presents successfully the three act drama of selling must possess and use imagination. The imagination is the workshop of the mind, in which is fashioned every idea, plan, and mental picture with which the salesman creates desire in the mind of his prospective buyer. Salesmen whose imaginations are deficient, resemble a ship without a rudder—they go round and round in circles and finish where they started, without making a favorable impression.

Words alone, will not sell!

Words, woven into combinations of thought which create desire, will sell. Some salesmen never learn the difference between rapid-fire conversation which does not end soon enough and carefully painted word-pictures which fire the imagination of the prospective buyer.

The sole object of neutralizing the mind of prospective buyers is, of course, to establish confidence. Where confidence has not been first built in the mind of the prospect, no sale can be made.

THE TEN MAJOR FACTORS ON WHICH CONFIDENCE IS BUILT

By careful observation of thousands of sales people from whom I have learned all that I know about selling, I discovered that ten major factors enter into the development of confidence. They are:

1. *Follow the habit of rendering more service and better service than you are paid to render.*
2. *Enter into no transaction that does not benefit, as nearly alike as possible, everyone it affects.*
3. *Make no statement which you do not believe to be true, no matter what the temporary advantages a falsehood might seem to offer.*
4. *Have a sincere desire in your heart to be of the greatest possible service to the largest number of people.*
5. *Cultivate a wholesome admiration for people; like them better than you like money!*
6. *Do your best to live as well as preach your own philosophy of business. Actions speak louder than words!*
7. *Accept no favors, large or small, without giving favors in return.*

8. ***Ask nothing of any person without believing that you have a right to that for which you ask.***
9. ***Enter into no arguments with any person over trivial or non-essential details.***
10. ***Spread the sunshine of good cheer wherever and whenever you can. No man trusts a joy-killer!***

This list is well worth memorizing. It is also worth following.

A Master Salesman can sell a man anything he needs if the purchaser has confidence in the salesman.

He can also sell a man many things that he does not need, *but he doesn't*. Remember, a Master Salesman plays the double role of buyer and seller. He therefore does not try to sell any person anything which he, himself, would not buy if he were actually in the position of the prospective buyer.

There is a well-known type of crook who is a Master Salesman. He is known as a *confidence man*. His sole equipment is his ability to build confidence in the minds of his victims. His stealings run into the millions, and his victims may be found among the shrewdest of business men, professional men and bankers.

These crooks often "stalk" their victims for months, or even years, for the purpose of building a relationship of perfect coincidence. When this foundation has been properly laid, the smartest men may be "taken in." Men are without defense against those in whom they have perfect confidence.

If confidence can be used successfully as the sole tool of operation of the crook, surely it can be used with greater effect for legitimate business and professional purposes. The salesman who knows how to build a bridge of confidence between himself and his prospective purchasers may write his own income-ticket, as all such salesmen do.

High-pressure methods, exaggerated statements of fact, willful misrepresentation, whether by direct statement or by innuendo, destroy confidence.

A little while ago, one of the biggest sales producers in the employ of a well-known automobile dealer was let out of his position at the end of the most successful sales month he had ever experienced. He was dismissed because a check-up of his accounts with the finance company disclosed the fact that more than three-fourths of his customers had lapsed in their payments. A further check-up disclosed the fact that this so-called salesman had high-pressured his buyers into signing orders by telling them that if anything happened which made it inconvenient for them to make their monthly payments promptly, they could skip a couple of months or so without jeopardizing their rights. The automobile agency for which this man worked lost prestige through his acts which it will never be able to regain.

Every successful business firm must have the confidence of its patrons. The salesman is intermediary through which this confidence is acquired, or he may be the medium through which it is lost. The Master Salesman, knowing as he does, the importance of acquiring and holding the confidence of his buyers, bargains with them as if he were the owner of the business he represents. He deals with his customers exactly as he would want them dealt with if he were, in fact, the owner of the business.

Confidence is the basis of all harmonious relationships. The salesman who overlooks this fact is unfortunate; he can never become a Master Salesman. This means he limits his earning capacity and circumscribes his possibilities of advancement.

In the city of Chicago, a Master Salesman conducts a chain of men's hat stores. Some twenty years ago, when these stores were first brought to my attention, they specialized in Two Dollar hats. The hats were sold with the guarantee that if the customer found his purchase unsatisfactory, he could bring back the hat, or any part of it, to the store and receive a brand new one in its place with no questions asked.

I was informed by the owner of the store that one man had even been coming back twice a year, for more than seven years, and exchanging his old hat for a new one.

"And you permit him to get away with that?" I inquired. "Get away with it?" the store owner replied, "Why, man alive! If I had a hundred men doing the same thing, I could retire from business with all the money I need, inside of five years. Never a day passes that we do not trace sales to the talking done by this man. He is literally a walking and a talking advertisement for us."

That statement threw an entirely different light on the subject. I saw that this hat store owner had built an enormous business upon an unusual policy which developed confidence.

There are two major occasions which cause men and women to talk, and, therefore, advertise favorably or unfavorably a business; when they think they have been cheated, and when they have received a fairer treatment than expected.

All people are like this. They are impressed by the law of contrast. Anything unusual or unexpected, whether it impress favorably or unfavorably, makes a lasting impression.

*   *   *   *   *

"Whatever you possess, material, mental, or spiritual, you must use it or lose it!"
                              – Napoleon Hill

*   *   *   *   *

CHAPTER 12
The Art Of Closing A Sale

The climax, or closing of a sale is said to be the most difficult part of the entire transaction. This is not true, however, if the ground-work leading to the close has been properly laid. The climax of a sale is a mere detail *if* a sale has been properly made.

In almost every instance when a sale is hard to close, the difficulty may be found in some part of the transaction preceding the climax. Before trying to reach a climax, the Master Salesman prepares the way carefully, step by step, through proper attention to the following important details.

(a) Has he taken care to neutralize the mind of his prospect to make it receptive to his sales presentation.

(b) He has made the mind of his prospect favorable by establishing confidence.

(c) He has qualified the prospect's mind accurately to make sure that he is dealing with a prospect and not a mere "suspect"

(d) *Above all he has planted in the prospect's mind the most logical motive for buying.*

(e) He has tested the prospect, during his sales presentation, and has made sure that the prospect followed his presentation with keen interest. This he has accomplished by keen observation of the prospect's facial expression and his statements denoting a desire for the object of the sale.

(f) Last, but by no means least, the salesman has *made the sale in his own mind before trying to reach a climax!* He knows this by the "feel" of his prospect's mind. No one can become a Master Salesman without developing the ability to "tune in" on the prospect's mind through the sixth sense. This ability, more than anything else, is the distinguishing feature of a Master Salesman.

Having taken these steps satisfactorily, the salesman is now ready to reach terminal facilities to close the sale. There are thousands of salesmen who can arouse interest, the first step in the actual process of selling; and create a desire for their wares, the second step; but at the third step they fall down because the lack the ability to close! Let it be remembered, however, that if the six detailed steps described in this book have been properly taken, the close comes easily and is nothing but a mere detail.

GUIDELINES FOR CLOSING A SALE

The following suggestions will be helpful, even to the seasoned salesman, in developing mastery in closing:

1. Do not permit your prospect to lead you away from your sales plan by engaging in argument over non-essentials or extraneous subjects. If your prospect insists upon breaking in while you are talking and tries to direct the conversation so as to build up a defensive alibi for not buying, let him go along until he exhausts himself; then tactfully switch him back to your own trend of thought the moment he hesitates. Go right along and develop your own thoughts to the climax. This is absolutely essential. Either the salesman or the prospect dominates. It makes a great difference to the salesman which one does the dominating.

2. Anticipate negative questions and objections which you feel exist in your own prospect's mind, beat him to it. Ask and answer these questions yourself. Never bring up negative questions unless you are sure that your prospect has them in his mind. In selling it pays to "let sleeping dogs lie."

3. Always assume that your prospect is going to buy, no matter what he does or says to indicate the contrary, and let him know by every word and every movement that you expect him to buy. If you weaken on this point, you are beaten at the outset because your buyer may be shrewd enough to observe that you are not sure of yourself. If he does, he will use this as an alibi with which to give you a negative answer when you try to close. The Master Salesman *never* waivers for a moment and never shows the white feather, regardless of how clever the prospect may be at setting traps for the purpose of causing the salesman to weaken. Some of them are quite as clever at leading the salesman off the scent as the Master Salesman is at sticking to the trail of his argument. Be on the lookout for this sort of tactic and be prepared to negotiate successfully through the opposition of this nature.

4. Assume the attitude that your buyer is right; that he knows his business. Any suggestion that you may make by direct statement or by innuendo that you are smarter than he, will be sure to antagonize him, although he may not show his antagonism openly. The majority of mediocre salesmen make the mistake of trying to impress their prospect with their superior knowledge. This is usually poor salesmanship. It has cost more than one salesman the opportunity of making a sale.

5. When naming the amount of the purchase, set the figure high. It is better to come down in the amount, if you find that necessary, than it is to set the amount too low and then find yourself with no margin in which to trade when closing time comes. It is far better to start high and compromise by coming down, than it is to start low and then try to build up. Even if the figure you name is out of the prospect's financial range, your assumption of his ability to buy at the larger amount will not offend him.

If however, you make the mistake of underestimating his financial ability, you may offend. It has happened many times.

6. Use the question method to induce your prospect to commit himself on vital points out of which you intend to build your sales presentation. Then refer to those points as his own ideas! This is among the most effective of sales tactics, since a man will naturally uphold any statement which he has made (or thinks he has made).

7. If your prospective buyer says he wishes to consult his banker or his lawyer or his wife or some acquaintances whose opinion he values, congratulate him on his good judgement and his exercise of caution. Then begin at once to plant in his mind, through tactful suggestion, that while bankers may know the money-lending business, lawyers may understand the technicalities of the law, wives and friends may be well informed and loyal, the fact still remains that no one of them is apt to know as much about the wares you are offering as you yourself know. You have all the facts, while others have not and are not apt to take sufficient time or have sufficient interest to procure them. Moreover, plant the thought in the prospect's mind that, after all, he knows his own mind and his own business better than any other person.

8. Avoid permitting your prospect to think the matter over unless he has a very logical reason for the delay. When he springs that sort of alibi, pin him down and help him do the necessary thinking right then and there. Remember, an ounce of persistence at this point is worth a ton of cure afterward. The truth is, most sales which are lost could have been saved had the salesman been persistent for a few minutes longer.

WHEN IS THE PSYCHOLOGICAL MOMENT IN CLOSING

Much has been said about closing sales at the psychological moment, but experience has proved that the majority of salesmen do not know what the psychological moment is. The psychological moment is the time when the salesman feels that the prospect is ready to close. There is such a moment in every sale whether it be consummated or fails.

One of the major differences between a Master Salesman and a mediocre salesman is the Master Salesman's ability to sense what is in the prospect's mind, aside from what the buyer has expressed in actual words. The mediocre salesman is lacking in this keenness of perception through the sixth sense.

When you sense the psychological moment for closing, name the amount involved in the purchase and proceed to close the transaction right then. A delay of a few minutes, and often even a few seconds, may give the prospect a chance to change his mind. If you find, when you try to close your sale, that you have misjudged the psychological moment, go back over your sales presentation again, bringing in new closing arguments that you have saved for just such an emergency. You will need quite a stock of emergency arguments if you are to be placed in the category of Master Salesman.

No Master Salesman ever uses all of his trump cards unless he is forced to do so, and even then, he does not use them all at one time. He holds some back in case he has to make a secondary sales presentation to get the order.

The psychological moment for closing is something which the salesman usually has to sense, although there are times when that moment is obvious, either from the statements of the prospect or from his facial expressions. The salesman whose mind is negative or the salesman who is lacking in self-confidence often misses the feel of the psychological moment for closing, mistaking his own state of mind for that of his prospect.

On the other hand, this principle works in another way that is very advantageous to the salesman—the prospective buyer often mistakes the salesman's positive mind, self-confidence, and assurance of a willingness to buy for his own, and acts accordingly if the salesman insists upon closing the sale. If a salesman can transmit a negative thought to his prospective buyer (which he most assuredly can and does if he is not a Master Salesman), he can also transmit a positive thought; wherein may be found the real reason that the salesman should always assume an attitude both in manner and thought of belief that a sale will be consummated.

Eagerness to close a sale hurriedly, if observed by the prospective buyer, is generally fatal for the reason that eagerness to close is always accompanied by a lack of confidence on the part of the salesman, who transmits the thought to the mind of his prospect, if, in fact, he has not already disclosed his state of mind by his words and facial expression.

> **If the prospect gets the impression (no matter how he gets it) that the salesman is eager to make a sale because he (the salesman) needs the profit that is to be made on the sale, the chance of making the sale is usually spoiled. A salesman who carries an air of prosperity and nonchalance which reflects itself in his personal appearance and in the tone of his voice is usually a successful closer! The reason is obvious.**

A Master Salesman seldom asks the prospect if he is ready to close. He goes right ahead and at the psychological moment makes out the order, conducting himself in every way as if the question of the sale were settled. Asking the prospect if he is ready to close is the equivalent of expressing doubt that he is. But making out the order and handing it to the prospective buyer, leaves no doubt as to the salesman's state of mind on this subject. The buyer usually acts favorably upon such a positive suggestion, provided, of course, that the sales presentation has been properly made and the desire to buy has been planted in the prospects mind.

Remember always that the place for a salesman to close a sale is first of all in his own mind. The whole world stands aside and makes room for the man who knows exactly what he wants and has made up his mind to have just that. Let a man hesitate and by that hesitation express lack of confidence and the crowd will walk all over his toes. The salesman who reflects the slightest sign of hesitancy or doubt when the closing time comes, may as well not ask for the order; he is almost sure to meet with a refusal.

This is the way men's minds work!

It is important that one be able to realize where a sale potentially exists and follow to successful conclusion situations which might not have been obviously declaring, "Here is a sale!"

Ray Cunliffe, the Baltimore distributor of the Cadillac automobile, told me a typical case of a salesman who unwittingly tried to register a "no sale" that almost cost him the commissions on three expensive automobiles. The incident took place in the New York Sales Room of the old Locomobile Company.

Late one afternoon just before closing time (the five o'clock variety), a rather sportily dressed man walked into the sales room and told the floor man that he was interested in a Locomobile. Three new cars were standing on the floor. The man balanced himself on his cane and looked at all three cars for a few minutes then asked the price. In a very indifferent attitude the floor man told him, but made no effort to give his prospective buyer the "works." The price of the cars, as I recall it, was $12,000.00 each.

The sportily dressed gentleman stood and looked at the cars a minute or two. Then he said (pointing to each car as he spoke), "Well, I do not know whether I will take this one, or this one, or this one or whether I will take all three of them."

That settled the matter. The man was a Broadway crank. Moreover, the salesman had a dinner appointment and was in a hurry to get away. Luckily, before his "no sale" mental attitude had had time to register in the prospect's mind, the man said, "I see you are anxious to get away, so I guess I will take this car," pointing to the one which stood in the middle of the floor.

"All right," the salesman replied, "I will help you fill out an order."

"Oh, never mind about an order blank," the prospective buyer answered, "I will just give you my check for the car and you can send it out to my home tomorrow." Meanwhile he took out his checkbook, and wrote a check for $12,000.00 and handed it to the floor man.

As soon as the floor man saw the name on the check, his face turned three different shades of red. The signature was that of Charles Payne Whitney, who, as the floor man well knew, could have been *sold* all three

Quibbling over salary "to start with" has lost many a person the big opportunity of a lifetime. If the position you seek is one that you know you can throw your whole heart into, take it, even if you have to work for nothing until you deliver a good sample of your "goods." Thereafter you will receive pay in proportion to the quality and quantity of the work you perform.

cars just as easily as the one he purchased. Observe that the word I used was "purchased"; no *sale* was made in that case.

Some time ago, I sent out word to several real estate men that I was in the market for property in the country and described in detail the sort of place I wanted. Salesmen came by the score. I never knew before how many men were trying to make a living by selling real estate. That they were all hungry for business was plainly indicated by their eagerness to "put me on the spot."

I said that scores of "salesmen" came. Perhaps it would be more in keeping with the facts if I said that *a* salesman came, for out of the entire lot there was but one man who understood the psychology of closing. Most of them described their property by showing me maps and the like. Some of them handed me printed literature describing it and asked me to look it over and let them know when I was ready to see the property. How did they know I was not then ready?

Not one of them had the initiative to invite me out to see their property with the exception of the one salesman who came. This man said, "We have just the place your letter described. We have been holding it for you for a long time (winking to show that he was taking a slight liberty with my credulity). Jump in my car and we will run out and see your property. If it is not exactly what you want, I will buy you the best dinner in the city when we return." (He had enough imagination to observe that it would be about time for dinner upon our return.) "When you see this place," he continued, "you will look no further. I am sure it is just what you want."

By that time I had begun to believe that he knew what I wanted. He had caused me to do something I had not intended to do, namely, to inspect the property that day. His whole demeanor was so positive and assured that I found myself in his car before I had a chance to think of a good reason for not going. If he had hesitated in his approach, I could have put him off until the following day, but it was his business, doubtless, to strike while the iron was hot, so I was on my way in less time than it takes to tell the story.

On the way this salesman described the place so accurately and so pleasingly that I almost felt myself the owner of it before I had seen it.

Frankly, I would have been greatly disappointed to find anything wrong with it, because the salesman had planted the seed of desire in my mind so deeply that I was like putty in his hands.

The salesman took the contract with him and got my name on the dotted line before we left the property. It was one of the smoothest pieces of salesmanship I have ever observed. The moment this salesman sensed that I was ready to sign, he took out his contract and handed it to me with his pen. Seeing that I had nothing on which to rest the contract while signing, he rushed to his car and pulled out a briefcase, saying, "Here, use this for a table, General!" Now, I am not a general, but the title was slipped to me so unobtrusively that I did not resent it.

And I signed!

This salesman handed me no literature to read over. He handed me the property instead. Master Salesmen always do something like that. It is one of their peculiarities.

Some of the other "salesmen" are still sending me printed literature *through the mail.* Now, if a country place was ever sold by printed literature alone, I should like to hear about it. The salesman who turned the trick must have been a miracle worker.

A few days ago one of these "salesmen" came in to see me. He wanted to know if I had "made up my mind about that country place I was looking for some time ago."

"Bless your life, yes," I replied, "perhaps I should say, however, that I did not make up my mind to buy it. A very able salesman made it up for me the same day that you first came to see me and made the sale that very day."

"That's too bad!" the "salesman" exclaimed.

"No," I replied, "it is only one bad. It may be bad for you, but it was fine for me because I got just the place I was looking for."

With a look on his face, which indicated that he vaguely suspected that I might be kidding him, this dilatory "salesman" turned and walked away without saying goodbye. He was obviously disgusted at my sense of humor or my credulity in buying a place the first time I saw it. I do not know which.

You cannot tell how far a frog can jump by counting the warts upon its back. No more can you tell, by merely looking at a prospect, whether you can sell him your wares. Give yourself the benefit of the doubt and give every prospect the "works" before registering a no sale in your own mind. It is the safest plan!

I once trained a sales army of 3,000 men and women for a Chicago firm. Efficiency had to be the watch word. We inaugurated a system from which I learned much about the possibilities of persistence! Before any salesman was permitted to become permanently allied with the organization, it was necessary for him to sell one out of the first five prospective buyers called upon. The instructions were to stick to these five prospects until a sale had been made. On many occasions salesmen called on those prospects as many as a dozen times before the sale was consummated.

I recall that one salesman called on one of his prospects eighteen times before he made a sale. The "victim" succumbed on the eighteenth visit and made a purchase out of self-defense. In the group of 3,000 sales people only 128 failed to qualify for permanent positions because they could not make a sale to the first five prospects called upon. We taught these sales people that "no" need not be taken seriously. Moreover, we proved it!

It was also apparent that confidence must be manifested by the salesman as well as by the prospect before a sale can be effected. To make sure that our sales people acquired confidence, we resorted to a very unique plan at the outset, that of setting up "dummy" offices, maintained by the company and managed by company employees. When we felt sure that a green salesman lacked only the quality of confidence in himself, we included in the list of the first five prospects the name of one of these "dummy" managers, who was instructed to give the salesman a hard battle, but to let him win by making a sale. These sales went through and commissions were paid on them. The effect was astounding, especially in the cases of sales people who had never tried to sell before.

We usually had the salesman call on the dummy buyer last, after the four legitimate prospects had been called on. We found, too, by experimenting, that after making the sale to the dummy, the effect was so encouraging that we could then send him back over the list of the four who had not been sold, with the result that in some instances all four of them were sold, despite the fact that they had previously failed.

We discovered, from this experimentation, that the salesman's state of mind has more to do with determining whether a sale is made than the state of mind of the prospective buyer. It is an important discovery, as true today as when it was made.

Were I asked to give a summation to these varied and often detailed examinations of the subject of selling, I believe I could do it in one word.

There is a word which should stand out upon the horizon of every salesman's vision, like Mars blazing at eventide, always there to be seen, challenging, beckoning, urging, inspiring, commanding.

The word denotes that thing which dominates all great and able sales people everywhere and it is a word which Edward Bok declared was the greatest in the English language. It is

SERVICE

*   *   *   *   *

"If you are successful remember that somewhere, sometime, someone gave you a lift or an idea that started you in the right direction. Remember also, that you are indebted to life until you help some less fortunate person, just as you were helped."

– Napoleon Hill

*   *   *   *   *

PART TWO

A NEGATIVE MIND SPAWNS ONLY NEGATIVE IDEAS

"It is a physical impossibility for a negative mind to generate positive thoughts. When you allow yourself to dwell on the negative aspects of life, negative thinking expands to fill all of your thoughts until there is no room for positive thoughts to grow. It becomes an endless cycle. The habit of negative thinking generates more and more negative thoughts, which the mind attempts to turn into physical reality. The result is a life of despair and hopelessness. Develop the habit of eliminating negative thoughts the moment they appear. Start small at first. When you first hear that inner voice that says, 'I can't do this,' put the thought out of your mind immediately. Instead, concentrate on the task itself. Break it down into manageable parts and complete them one at a time. When the job is finished, tell your doubting self: 'You were wrong. I could do it, and I did!'"

— **Napoleon Hill**

CHAPTER 13
Choosing Your Job

You have the privilege of choosing any position you desire, as an objective toward which to work! The making of this choice is the first step you must take in marketing your services effectively. Moreover, it is a responsibility which you alone must assume, as no other person can satisfactorily make the choice for you.

Before deciding what position or calling you desire, decide whether you merely want *a* position or *the* position for which you are best fitted by desire, education, temperament, and native ability.

The next decision to be made is that of determining whether you prefer a position that offers great opportunity in the future, with modest pay at the start or one which yields the maximum amount of pay, but offer no promise for the future. In other words, you must decide whether you wish to start at the top or at the bottom of the ladder.

Upon this decision depends to a large extent the ultimate amount of your earning capacity, since it is obvious that one who starts at the top can move in only one direction.

FACTORS WHICH SHOULD INFLUENCE YOUR CHOICE OF OCCUPATION

Observe with profit the frequency with which the word decision appears throughout this book. The marketing of personal service, in an effective manner, calls for many decisions. The following are factors which enter into the marketing of Personal Services in connection with which you must reach decisions.

1. Decide which calling or occupation you like best. Careful analysis of many thousands of men and women has shown that one experiences the greatest and most enduring success when engaged in the work which one likes best. When one enters into that sort of work, it is with enthusiasm and zeal akin to that employed when playing a game. No person should voluntarily choose an occupation into which he does not feel he can throw his whole heart and soul.

2. Decide what type of employer you prefer. It is just as important for you to choose your employer with care as it is for the employer to choose his employees with care. In your choice of an employer, pick one in whom you have confidence and from whose example of conduct you may benefit. Choose one from whom you may gather useful knowledge connected with the occupation of your choice. Your employer should become, as he will in fact, your teacher. Be sure that the teacher is capable.

3. Decide the amount of money you intend to make your position yield year by year for the first five years. Then proceed to render service which will justify the amounts upon which you have decided. Remember that the amount of your annual earnings is the equivalent of 6 percent of the capital value of your brains. For example, if your income is $6,000.00 a year, you have in your brain, capital the equivalent of $100,000.00. Regard this capital as something which must be kept at work efficiently if you are to collect the income.

4. Decide—and this decision is most important—exactly the quality and the quantity of service you intend to deliver in return for the income you expect to demand and deliver at least that—no less! The majority of people devote more time to thinking about the money they want or need than they do about creating ways and means of earning that amount through an equivalent of service.

5. Decide to what extent you are handicapped by the major causes of failure and select an occupation which will be conducive to the elimination of that handicap. (These Major Causes are explained in the author's book *Think and Grow Rich.*)

These five decisions must be made before you are ready to create a plan for marketing your services. They constitute five of the most important decisions you will ever be called upon to make. Reach them promptly, but with due thought and deliberation because your whole future depends upon the sort of decisions you make.

If you are just starting out in search of your first position, it will be permissible for you to accept temporary employment such as you may need for living expenses until you have had time to gather the information required to make these five decisions intelligently. Do not make the mistake of permitting your temporary employment to become your life-work because of indifference or habit. Ninety-eight per cent of the people of the world may be considered failures from the viewpoint of earnings and occupation. Also, ninety-eight per cent of the people holding positions have drifted into them and remained there because they lacked the power of decision to choose more suitable positions.

One of the most pathetic sights I have ever witnessed is that of a man who has committed himself to the wearisome treadmill of toil for his entire lifetime, where he must spend six days out of every seven at labor which he does not like. Such a man is in a prison to which he has sentenced himself for a term approximating six-sevenths of his life. Moreover, he is no less a prisoner than the man who is behind bars, the only difference being that he has a slightly wider scope of freedom one day out of every seven.

Performing labor which one does not like is one of the great tragedies of civilization. Stating the case conversely, voluntary choice of an occupation, which one does like and into which one may throw himself wholeheartedly, requires greater willpower and more force of character than the average person is disposed to exercise. Observe with significance that I did not say more force of character than the average person possesses. Possession of personal power and use of it are two different things.

The reason one should choose an occupation which one likes is obvious. Service rendered in connection with an occupation which one enjoys is never burdensome toil, because it is a form of labor which one enjoys. You get tired, not from over-work, but from lack of interest in what you are doing.

Here is an appropriate place at which to reply to the person who asks, "How can I avoid engaging in labor which I do not like?" The answer is, you can avoid it by firmly *deciding* you will not become a prisoner for life in a prison of your own making. Or, if you find yourself temporarily in such a prison because of the necessity of living, you can release yourself by deciding that you are going to select another occupation and then follow that decision with action in harmony with the instructions described in this book.

The book was written with the primary ideas of serving as a key by which men and women may release themselves from prisons of labor which they do not like. It will serve as such a key for all who follow it.

We are all creatures of habit!

We are where we are and what we are because of the habits of which we have become the victims, voluntarily or involuntarily. We are victims of the habits of thought and the habits of action. We can change our station in life—and this is the only way we can change it—by changing our habits.

You might as well know here and now that you cannot hope to market your personal services more advantageously without changing your present habits. If your habits were constructive, there would be neither the desire nor the necessity for you to concern yourself about marketing your personal services differently.

SOMETHING FOR NOTHING

Life has no bargain counters. Everything has a price which must be paid in one form or another. No man is smart enough to cheat Life. It has been tried by the smartest of men without success.

The price of success in marketing personal services is measured in a great variety of terms and equivalents, all of which have been plainly described in this book. Familiarize yourself with these price tags and decide if you are willing to pay the price.

If you are reading this book in the hope that it may explain some plan of "hocus-pocus" by which you may sell your services for more than they are worth, lay this book down right now. On the other hand, if you want money in greater quantities than you are now receiving and are prepared to give in return an equivalent of service, this book will guide you safely over the pitfalls and mistakes which even the most sincere sometimes make..

> **This is an age when the predominating tendency of man is to get without giving! That tendency toward avarice and greed is in the very air and you will become the victim of it by the example of others around you, if you do not watch yourself.**

I am trying to emphasize this for the benefit of young people who have not yet become the victims of the victims of this mad desire for something for nothing. I qualify my statement to apply to young men and women because I know that but few, if any, of the older ones whose habits have become fixed, will pay any attention to this warning.

Nature balances her books and asks for an accounting every so often. When the accounting time comes, as it always does, those who have been lucky enough to acquire temporary possession of something for which they have not paid full value are forced to disgorge.

This rule applies to the delivery of personal services just as to all other transactions. One may get by for a time by rendering services which are inadequate in quality and quantity, but Nature's auditor awaits such a person just around the corner.

This chapter may appear to be just a dry preachment of the morals of salesmanship of personal services because truth is often less romantic than fiction! To all who so consider this chapter, I would offer the suggestion that it conforms perfectly to the rules of conduct which have been followed, consciously or unconsciously, by every man who has accumulated and kept a great fortune.

The lives of all successful people are controlled and guided by rules of conduct which are exacting and often devoid of romance. Before leaving this chapter, make one more decision. Would you prefer instructions which are sound and helpful, but free from fiction, or those which are optimistic, fictional, romantic, and unsound?

This book was not written with the purpose of describing how easy it is to receive big money by rendering inadequate service, but for the purpose of describing definite ways of earning money by rendering its equivalent in *satisfactory* service.

I am, by nature, an optimist! I would not rob labor of its romance if I could do so. To me, there is nothing more romantic in life than a man and a job which are suited to one another. Happiness is the ultimate height toward which every human being is striving. If life offers anything which will bring more happiness than the privilege of rendering useful service one enjoys, I do not know what it is.

Millions of people are out of employment and other millions realize from their labor barely enough for existence. Out of this experience have come many helpful lessons, among them the sure knowledge that there is one thing worse than being forced to labor. *It is being forced not to labor!*

No man can be happy without some form of occupation. Many have tried to find happiness in idleness. They have failed. Enduring happiness comes through serving. All other forms of happiness are transitory and delusive.

Happiness Comes From Aspiring, Not From Acquiring

No man can be happy in whose heart there is not the hope of achievement yet unattained. Men who have millions of dollars in wealth find no happiness in wealth. If they are happy, the happiness comes from aiming, hoping, creating and building plans for future achievement. I know of no exception to this rule, despite that fact that I have a personal acquaintance with scores of men of great wealth.

I am trying, as you may have observed, not merely to show you how to market your Personal Services effectively, but how to find happiness through your efforts, as well.

*   *   *   *   *

"I refuse to believe what you say unless it harmonizes with what you do!"

— **Napoleon Hill**

*   *   *   *   *

CHAPTER 14

Selecting A Definite Major Aim As Your Life Work

Singleness of purpose is a quality without which no one may attain to outstanding success. This is an age of specialization. It is also an age of keen competition which does not favor the person who cannot excel in some specific occupation.

THE FIVE FUNDAMENTAL STEPS TO YOUR SUCCESS

There are five fundamental steps that must be taken by all who succeed. They are:

1. *Choice of a definite goal to be attained*
2. *Development of sufficient power to attain one's goal*
3. *Perfection of a practical plan for attaining one's goal*
4. *Accumulation of specialized knowledge necessary for the attainment of one's goal*
5. *Persistence in carrying out your plan*

Every successful person follows, in one form or another, this five-step program. Some follow it unconsciously or by accident, while others follow it with a definite purpose and by design.

SOME OF THE ADVANTAGES OF A DEFINITE AIM

Working with definiteness of purpose toward a single goal has many advantages, among them the following:

FIRST: **Singleness of purpose forces one to specialize and specialization tends toward perfection.**

SECOND: **A definite goal permits one to develop the capacity to reach decisions quickly and firmly.**

THIRD: **Definiteness of purpose enables one to master the habit of procrastination.**

FOURTH: **Definiteness of purpose saves the time and energy one would otherwise waste while wavering between two or more possible courses of action.**

FIFTH: **A definite purpose serves as a road-map which charts the direct route to the end of one's journey.**

SIXTH: **Definiteness of purpose fixes one's habits so that they are taken over by the sub-conscious mind and used as a motivating force (involuntarily) in driving toward one's goal.**

SEVENTH: **Definiteness of purpose develops self confidence and attracts the confidence of other people.**

Disadvantages follow and blast the lives of those who have no clearly defined purpose." The purposeless lives and wrecked fortunes of a tragic host along the colorless shores of every sea whereon human endeavor has been launched, speak of millions without objectives who have held to no fixed goal. Drifting people are like rudderless ships and "all the voyages of their lives are bound in shallows and miseries."

Every cluttered tenement bears tragic evidence of this truth. Weak, pale and undernourished children who have never stood straight-limbed and fair in God's sunshine convince us of this truth. Women, pinched of face, poorly clad and with worried eyes, who have not time to look up from their dismal drudgery, mutely tell us of husbands without purpose.

Restless and scowling men, are they who have not *one* great goal. Truth, naked and undeniable, points an accusing finger at the shambles of human figures who know not where they go or why.

The North star was not more fixed in the heavens than Caesar in his purpose. History is rich in the recital of men who have hitched their wagon to a star—a single star—and ridden it into the heights of great achievement.

Great men in ages gone have given us words to be used as symbols to guide us on our way. But no words should be graven so high in the sky, there to arrest the attention of young men and young women, challenge their consideration, and bring them to a state of thoughtful reflection as these words *quo animo* (with what mind or intention).

Those who know where they are going usually get there. They do not dissipate their strength in aimless expenditure of time and energy, following first one course and then another, but concentrate their efforts upon a definite objective, exerting all powers to attain that end.

Brawn brings a daily wage. The price of it is fixed by the law of supply and demand. "General" services, rendered by one who has not specialized, brings but little more than brawn. Brains, when marketed through a definite aim have no fixed price. The sky is the limit in the marketing of specialized talent. These are statements of obvious fact, yet ninety-eight out of every hundred people fail all through life because they do not follow the principle of working with definiteness of purpose.

*　*　*　*　*

> *Every failure will teach you a lesson that you need to learn if you will keep your eyes and ears open and be willing to be taught. Every adversity is usually a blessing in disguise. Without reverses and temporary defeat, you would never know the sort of metal of which you are made.*
>
> **– Napoleon Hill**

*　*　*　*　*

CHAPTER 15

The Habit Of Doing More Than You Are Paid For

The habit of rendering more service and better service than one is paid to render is an absolute essential to the advantageous marketing of personal services.

In the previous chapter your attention was called to the importance of the word *decision!* In this chapter your attention is directed to the word *habit*, especially as it applies to the amount and quality of service rendered.

Among the many sound reasons for rendering more service and better service than expected are the following:

1. This habit turns the spotlight of favorable attention upon those who develop it.

2. This habit enables one to profit by the law of contrast, since the majority of people have conformed and apply the opposing habit, by rendering as little service as they can.

3. This habit gives one the benefit of the law of Increasing Returns and insures one against the disadvantages of the law of Decreasing Returns, thus eventually enabling one to receive more pay than one would receive without this habit.

4. This habit insures one preferred employment at preferred wages and permanency of employment as long as there is employment to be had. The person who practices this habit is the last to be removed from the payroll when business is poor and the first to be taken back after a layoff.

5. This habit develops greater skill, efficiency, and also greater earning ability and tends to give one preference over others.

6. This habit makes one practically indispensable to one's employer because it is a habit not to be found in the majority of people, and because it induces employers to relegate greater responsibilities to those who practice it. The capacity to assume responsibility is the quality that brings the highest monetary returns.

7. This habit leads to promotion because it indicates that those who practice it have ability for supervision and leadership not found in those who follow the opposite habit.

8. This habit enables one to set one's own salary. If it cannot be obtained from one employer, it may be obtained from his competitor.

These are but a few of the major advantages of rendering more service and better service than one is paid to render.

If you render no more service than you are paid to render, then it is obvious you are not entitled to any more pay. This is a fact against which there is no argument!

Every business has either a potential or a real asset known as good will. While this is an asset not generally listed in the inventory as such, it is, nevertheless, an asset without which no business can grow and but few, if any, businesses can exist for any great length of time. An individual who renders more service and better service than paid for many also have a good will asset which will assure him opportunities and advantages in connection with the sale of personal services which are not available to the person who does not practice this habit. This "good will" asset is generally known as one's *reputation* for efficiency. It is an asset without which no individual can market his personal services to best advantage.

The strongest and most attractive selling feature any individual may have, in marketing his personal services, is the habit of rendering service which is greater in quantity and superior in quality.

The habit of rendering more service and better service than one agrees to render for a stipulated sum is one of the most important principles through which businesses grow to huge proportions and businessmen accumulate great fortunes. The principle works in behalf of an employer just as it does in behalf of an employee, a fact which a few employers have discovered.

Men become harmonious, loyal, and cooperative in their efforts because of motive. Men who achieve outstanding success, whether as individuals or as the heads or business enterprises, understand how to attract the qualities of harmony, loyalty and cooperation through appropriate motive.

Every individual who works for a salary naturally wants more money and a better position. Not every such individual, however, understands that better positions and greater pay come as the result of motive and that the greatest of all motives with which these desirable benefits may be attracted is that of rendering more service and better service than one is paid to render.

YOUR GREATEST OPPORTUNITY
MAY BE RIGHT WHERE YOU ARE

It is man's inherent nature to seek what he believes to be greener pastures in the distance. When a man begins to look for a better position and more pay he usually seeks opportunity in the distance with some other employer. Sometimes this may be necessary, but changes in employment, while they may bring advantages, always bring some disadvantages, the most outstanding of which is the fact that one is never as efficient in a new position, a new environment, among new associates as he is where he is familiar with the details of his work and has the confidence of his associates. Moreover, the changing of positions deprives an individual of much of the good will value built around himself through long association with an employer.

Before deciding to change employers be sure that you have exhausted the possibilities of your present position. Take inventory of your job and ascertain in what ways you can make yourself more valuable to your employer. Follow this practice until you have made yourself as nearly indispensable to him as possible; remembering meanwhile that indispensability is the only thing behind which you can successfully hedge when you ask your employer for a better position or more pay.

If your employer is a successful businessman, he is probably also intelligent. He has the ability to approximate your value to his business. Before you make demands for more pay, or seek opportunity elsewhere, be sure that you are worth more by having first practiced the habit of rendering more service and better service than your employer had expected or demanded of you. If you have followed this habit long enough for your employer to have observed that it is a habit, you are in a position to ask him to discuss readjustment of your salary. You are not likely to suffer if your employer is successful and intelligent.

People sometimes outgrow both their positions and their employers. More often, however, the reverse proves true.

Before deciding to change employers, take inventory of your employer and his business. Ascertain whether or not they offer you a future commensurate with your ability. If the analysis shows that an adequate opportunity exists where you are, develop that opportunity. You already have your foot inside the door. You have your employer's confidence or you would not be where you are. Capitalize this opportunity by making yourself indispensable and very soon the law of increasing returns will begin to reward you.

Every competent farmer understands and makes use of the law of increasing returns. He puts this law into operation in the following manner:

FIRST: He selects soil which is appropriate for the crop which he expects it to yield.

SECOND: He then prepares this soil by plowing and harrowing and perhaps by fertilization, so it will be favorable to the seed he plants.

THIRD: He plants seed which has been carefully selected for soundness, knowing that poor seed cannot yield a bountiful crop.

FOURTH: He then gives Nature a chance to compensate him for his labor through an appropriate period of time. He does not sow the seed one day and expect to reap a harvest the next.

Having taken these four steps, all of which have been in advance of his reward, the farmer knows that he will profit by the law of increasing returns when harvest time arrives and that he will get back from his labor not merely the amount of seed he planted in the soil, but a greatly increased quantity.

Marketing personal services effectively involves this same principle. Prepare carefully the soil in which you intend to plant the seed of service by selecting an employer who is intelligent and successful. Then cultivate that soil and prepare it through conduct which is *harmonious* and *coopera-tive*. Plant in the soil the finest seed of service and be sure to plant an abundance of that seed as not all seed will germinate and grow. Do not expect to harvest a crop of pay before you have sown the seed of service. After the seed has been sown, do not become impatient if you do not reap your reward immediately. Give the seed time to germinate. Meanwhile you are making yourself indispensable to your employer and insuring permanency of employment.

If, after you have done your part, you employer does not show his appreciation, do not stop sowing the seed of service which is right in both quality and quantity. Keep right on sowing because it will provide you with the evidence of your capacity to render useful and desirable service if you find it necessary to seek employment elsewhere.

The habit of frequent changing of positions places an individual under the disadvantage of the law of *diminishing returns* because no employer wants to permit a rolling stone to become a factor in his business. This is worthy of application before you decide to change employers.

You are a merchant. You have the equivalent of a commodity to market. That equivalent is your personal services. Use the same principles of sound judgement in marketing your services that a successful merchant uses in marketing his merchandise. You know, of course, what happens to the merchant who short-weighs his customers or cheats them at trade. He pays by loss of business. You know, on the other hand, what happens to the merchant who builds confidence by rendering service and delivering merchandise which measures up to, or exceed the customer's expectations.

John Wanamaker, Marshall Field, and Sears-Roebuck built businesses which have become landmarks in American merchandising. Their motto

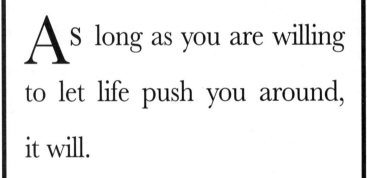

As long as you are willing to let life push you around, it will.

is: "The customer is always right," and they go to great extremes to make this motto mean what it says, even permitting some of their customers to take advantage of them in order to "teeth" into that policy.

No person may be sure of success, no matter what may be his calling, without applying this principle of giving before trying to get! Failure to apply this principle will render practically useless every other principle for the successful marketing of personal services.

Emphasis of this principle seems doubly necessary because of the prevailing tendency which obtains all over the world at this time to seek a harvest in wealth without first sowing the seed of service. The depression, which began in 1929, was a most impressive example of the existence of the law of diminishing returns. People went money mad and tried to get without giving through the law of chance. That law is tricky. It permits you to win just often enough to lure you on to sure destruction.

Every person whose major source of capital is his capacity to render personal services should remember the lesson taught by the depression and profit by it. From that experience came a worldwide demonstration that "He profits most who serves best."

During prohibition I visited a small town just across the border of Southern California in Mexico. I witnessed the spectacle of forty thousand men and women who had come across the line to patronize saloons and gambling halls. Except for the depression, I have never witnessed so huge a demonstration of man's lack of understanding of the futility of gambling. The experience aroused my curiosity and caused me to investigate for the purpose of understanding and ascertaining how well Lady Luck favored those forty thousand "go-getters" who were looking for something for nothing.

The government authorities in charge informed me that, by conservative estimate, less than three hundred of the forty thousand people who visit the town every Sunday go back over the border line with more money than they brought with them. The officials also estimated that the net value to the saloon keepers and gaming proprietors of a Sunday's business averaged about ten dollars per person or four hundred thousand dollars! They estimated that the three hundred who were lucky enough to go away with more than they brought, took away not to exceed twenty dollars each, or a total of six thousand dollars. Compare these two sums and you have about the percentage of opportunity one has of winning when one tries to get without giving!

The odds against the person who tries to get without giving an equivalent apply to the person who attempts to collect pay before delivering adequate service, just as they do to people who gamble. Those who try to harvest before sowing generally believe themselves wise enough to beat the game. It cannot be done. The business depression proved conclusively that the strongest men living, just like the small fry, fall and are crushed by this unsound belief.

Every person whose income is derived from the sale of personal services has occasional opportunity to cheat by delivering a shortage in quantity or deficiency in quality; but the cheater only cheats himself because this form of default is a mild method of stealing and those who practice it write the results indelibly into their own characters to be heard from later on.

Most men can cheat others occasionally without detection. But no man can cheat others without observation by his own *conscience* and that conscience is an official recorder of one's acts and thoughts. It writes the record of every thought and deed into the fabric of one's character.

A clear conscience is an asset comparable to no other!

You will discover this to be true when you come to the time when you wish to negotiate for the readjustment of your pay.

Master Salesmanship, regardless of the wares one may be selling, is based upon absolute faith in the thing one is offering for sale. Remember this when you bargain for the sale of your services.

*   *   *   *   *

"E. M. Statler became the mot successful hotel man in the world by rendering more service and better service than his guests were asked to pay for."

— Napoleon Hill

*   *   *   *   *

CHAPTER 16

Your Pleasing Personality

A major portion of your responsibility, regardless of your calling, is that of being able to negotiate your way through life with a minimum of friction between yourself and other people. To negotiate with others without friction is a rare ability. It is necessary in marketing personal services effectively.

A pleasing personality is an asset without which it is difficult to market personal services or to keep them marketed. Andrew Carnegie rated this quality at the head of the list of qualifications for success and went so far as to say that personality could often be substituted for brains. Perhaps Mr. Carnegie did not mean for that statement to be taken literally, but used it merely to emphasize the importance of a pleasing personality in marketing personal services.

Anyway, it is well worth thinking about.

The person who markets his or her services effectively must be an able salesman. A pleasing personality is an essential quality in salesmanship. Let us approach the study of this subject on a common ground of understanding by defining pleasing personality as follows:

A pleasing personality is one which has flexibility and adapt-ability sufficient to permit an individual to harmonize with any environment, and the necessary magnetism to dominate through attraction.

A pleasing personality consists of many qualities, the more important of which are:

1. ***Good showmanship.*** An efficient showman is one who

understands and applies the art of catering to the masses. He appeals to people through their imagination and keeps them interested through curiosity. A good showman is quick to recognize and to capitalize other people's prejudices, biases, likes, and dislike at the psychological moment.

2. ***Harmony within self.*** No one may enjoy a pleasing personality without first developing harmony and control within his own mind.

3. ***Definiteness of Purpose.*** The procrastinator who drifts through life without a plan or purpose can never be pleasing to others. To have a pleasing personality one must at least be definite in developing relationships of harmony with others and in adopting a major goal at which to aim as a life work.

4. ***Appropriateness of clothing.*** The person with a pleasing personality dresses in clothing which is appropriate not only to himself but also to his calling. First impressions are lasting. Inappropriate wearing apparel creates a prejudice which is difficult to overcome. Clothes may not "make the man," but they give him an advantageous start, if selected with taste.

5. ***Posture and carriage of the body.*** One does not have to be a character analyst to be able to judge other people by the way they walk and the general posture of their bodies. Alertness in posture and carriage of the body indicates alertness of the brain and keenness of perception.

6. ***Voice.*** The tone, volume, pitch, and general emotional coloring of one's voice constitute important factors of a pleasing personality. A high pitched voice is never pleasing; it is often offensive.

7. ***Sincerity of purpose.*** This quality needs but little, if any, explanation. Without it one may not have the confidence of others.

8. ***Choice of language.*** The man with a pleasing personality expresses himself in language appropriate to his calling and avoids the use of slang or profanity.

9. ***Poise.*** Poise is based upon self-confidence and self-control. Lack of it irritates and annoys other people.

10. ***A keen sense of humor.*** Perhaps no other quality is more essential than this. Without it one's life is a series of ups and downs—mostly downs!

11. ***Unselfishness.*** Selfishness and a pleasing personality are never found together. No one is attracted to a selfish person.

12. ***Facial expression.*** Facial expression is an accurate medium for the interpretation of one's moods and thoughts. It is the character analyst's barometer, by which he may measure accurately how one's mind functions.

13. ***Positive thought.*** Negative thoughts and a pleasing personality do not make good bedfellows because the vibrations of thought are picked up by others. Be sure, therefore, to release only such thoughts as will be pleasing to other people.

14. ***Enthusiasm.*** People who lack enthusiasm cannot arouse others. Enthusiasm is an essential factor in all forms of salesmanship, the sale of personal services included.

15. ***A sound body.*** Poor health does not attract people. Moreover, one cannot be enthusiastic without health and vigor. A bottle of citrate of magnesia or an internal bath would have saved many persons the loss of their positions.

16. ***Imagination.*** Alertness to the imagination is one of the most essential factors of a pleasing personality. Without it people are generally referred to as "dumb."

17. ***Tact.*** Lack of this quality has cost many men their positions to say nothing of their greatest opportunities. Lack of tact is usually expressed through loose conversation and boldness of expression.

18. ***Versatility.*** A general acquaintance with the important subjects of current interest and the deeper problems of life and living is a quality conducive to a pleasing personality.

19. ***The art of being a good listener.*** Train yourself to listen attentively when other people are speaking and do not show ill breeding by breaking in and taking the conversation away from others. Giver your ears a chance! Your tongue will take care of itself.

20. ***The art of forceful speech.*** No single factor of a pleasing personality is more important than this. Forceful speech is

the salesman's greatest asset. Without it, he is "sunk" before he begins to swim. It is an art which may be acquired by practice. The instructions for making an interesting speech are: Have something to say which is worth listening to and say it with all the enthusiasm at your command.

21. *Personal magnetism.* This term has reference to *controlled* sexual energy. It is the only factor of a pleasing personality which may not be acquired. One is either born with it or does not have it. Most people have it, but do not control it! It is the major asset of every great salesman and every leader in all walks of life. Its importance as a factor of a pleasing personality entitles it to appear at the head instead of the foot of the list.

This may appear to be a rather formidable list of qualities which one must possess in order to have a pleasing personality, but there is encouragement in the fact that the majority of these qualities may be had through practice plus definite determination to possess them.

As a part of your preparation as a salesman of your personal services, you should check yourself carefully against this list of factors of a pleasing personality, find out in which you are deficient, and begin at once to correct those deficiencies. You will find more explicit instructions for making this analysis in the chapter on Personal Analysis. You want all that your personal services can be marketed for, but you have no reason to expect your services to yield more than they are worth. Make them *worth* more. You can begin by rebuilding your personality. It is almost certain that you will find in this long list of factors which constitute a pleasing personality, some in which you are deficient. That is the place for you to begin rebuilding yourself!

A FEW WHO HAVE ACHIEVED SUCCESS THROUGH A PLEASING PERSONALITY

It may be helpful if you are reminded of some of the men who have risen to high places in life, not because of their superiority of education, but because they understood the art of selling themselves to advantage.

William Jennings Bryan kept himself sold to a large proportion of the

American people for more than thirty years almost solely upon his ability as an orator. Bryan was not a really great thinker. He was popular because of his ability to reach people through an appeal to their imaginations. The tone of his voice was responsible for much of his popularity.

Theodore Roosevelt kept himself well sold to the American people, in the highest position any American can hold, through almost two terms as President of the United States and just barely missed a third term. He was a great showman and an appealing public speaker, dynamic, energetic, powerful.

Will Rogers converted a pleasing personality into a huge fortune, through clowning. He was not a great actor but he acquired the ability to please people.

The late Knute Rockne developed the Notre Dame football team into the most popular team known to the American people. He was an able showman and possessed the ability to inject his personality into his players.

THE INFLUENCE OF PERSONALITY ON ATMOSPHERE

Every human being carries with him what is known as an "individual atmosphere." This atmosphere is but the sum total of an individual's reflection of the factors of a pleasing personality, plus any of the factors of a negative personality which the individual may possess. This atmosphere is contagious.

> **Every business and every place of employment has also a distinctive atmosphere which consists of the combined personalities of those who work there. A person with a dominating personality of pleasing nature may so color the atmosphere of the place where he works that the spirit of the entire place will also be pleasing. On the other hand, one person who has a dominating personality of a negative nature may transmit that personality to everyone in a place of business so that the atmosphere of the place becomes displeasing and unpleasant.**

Emerson had this truth in mind when he said, "Every business is the extended shadow of one person."

Remember that you are contributing through your personality to the atmosphere of the home in which you live and the place of business where you work. The feeling one gets when one walks into either the Marshall Fields Store in Chicago, or the John Wanamaker store in Philadelphia, is pleasing and attractive because of the positive atmosphere found in them. Every home carries an atmosphere which indicates clearly whether there is harmony or friction as the dominating factor of the home.

The positive or pleasing atmosphere value of a place of business, while it is an intangible asset, is one of the greatest assets any business can have. Such an atmosphere may be had only through a combination of positive individual personalities.

The man or women who carries a grouch into his place of employment does almost as much damage to his fellow employees, and to the business as might be done if poison were placed in the drinking water. Employers who understand this principle—and some of them do understand it—watch very carefully to see that only people with pleasing personalities work in their establishment.

THE MAJOR FACTORS OF A NEGATIVE PERSONALITY

We come now to examine the qualities which constitute a negative personality. Analyze and check yourself carefully by it to make sure that you are not unconsciously carrying around with you an atmosphere that causes people to dislike you. The list is as follows:

1. ***Disloyalty.*** There is no substitute for loyalty! The person who lacks loyalty is poverty-stricken, regardless of his other qualities or worldly possessions. Such a person cannot possibly market his personal services effectively because the market for those services will play out as soon as that quality is disclosed.

2. **Dishonesty.** There is no substitute for honesty! It is the key-stone to the arch of character. Without sound character no person can market his services effectively.

3. **Greed.** A person who is cursed by greed is never liked by others. It is a quality which cannot be kept under cover. It will assert itself so clearly that all may observe it and shun the person who reflects it.

4. **Envy and hatred.** These qualities make a pleasing personality an impossibility. Like attracts like. The person who hates people will in turn be hated by people, regardless of company manners or attempts to cover this disagreeable trait.

5. **Jealousy.** This is a mild form of insanity. It is fatal to a pleasing personality.

6. **Anger.** Whether passive or active in form, this is a quality which arouses antagonism and makes one disliked by others.

7. **Fear.** This quality repels people. It never attracts. There are Six Basic Fears against which every person must guard. These are negative states of mind which must be eliminated before one may develop a pleasing personality. Fear never pleases and it never attracts anything except its counterpart. (See the author's book *Think And Grow Rich.*)

8. **Revenge.** A revengeful person cannot be pleasing to anyone.

9. **Fault finding.** The person who has the habit of finding fault with others or with conditions cannot please. Such a person might more profitably spend his time looking within for faults.

10. **Peddling scandal.** The old saying that "a dog that will fetch a bone will take one back" is true. People may listen to the scandal-monger because they cannot avoid it, but they will not like the person.

11. **Uncontrolled enthusiasm.** Too much enthusiasm is a bad as none. Enthusiasm, controlled and directed, is generally more effective than that which is expressed too freely. No one is attracted to the person who "starts his tongue wagging and then goes off and leaves it."

12. **Prevarication.** The untruthful person is *persona non grata* in every household and in every place of business. With some people prevarication is a habit. It destroys confidence and sets up antagonism.

13. **Escaping responsibility for mistakes through alibis.** The alibi artist is never pleasing to others. It is better to assume responsibility for mistakes you do not make than to form the habit of trying to place responsibility for these mistakes on others.

14. **Exaggeration.** It is better to understate a truth than to overstate it. Exaggeration causes loss of confidence.

15. **Egotism.** Uncontrolled egotism is one of the most damaging of traits. There is but one form of egotism which is acceptable. It is the habit of expressing one's ideas in deeds helpful to others, not in words. Self-confidence is one of the most desirable and necessary traits, but it most be controlled and directed to definite ends, through methods which do not antagonize others. All forms of self-praise are easily recognized as evidences of inferiority complexes, therefore one's motto should be "deeds, not words."

16. **Obstinacy.** The person who is obstinate, stubborn, and self-willed is never pleasing. A certain amount of determination and the ability to stand by one's opinions is, of course, essential, but these qualities should not become a blanket policy.

17. **Selfishness.** No one likes a selfish person. This quality attracts opposition in every conceivable form.

These are not all of the negative qualities of personality, but they are, on the whole, the ones that do the most damage. Somewhere in the list you may find the cause of opposition which you may have experienced from others. You cannot have a pleasing personality until you put your foot upon the neck of every one of these signals of danger! Be merciless with yourself when you check yourself against this list, remembering that an enemy discovered is an enemy half conquered.

This chapter deals with subjects of a highly intimate personal nature. Remember when you step before the mirror of your own conscience, as you will if you derive real benefit from this chapter, that this book was not written as a sop to the vanity of any reader. It was written as a means of helping people to market their services effectively by first understanding and improving what they have to market.

Keep this thought clearly in mind and be your most severe critic as you read, if you wish to avail yourself of the benefits which await after you have mastered the principles described in this book. A pleasing personality is a self-acquired asset with but few exceptions. Its acquisition calls for self-control and a willingness to change destructive habits.

This book has been written with the object of helping people to convert their personal services into wealth without violating the rights or arousing the antagonism of others. This will, of course, require effort. Through your personal conduct you are establishing the limitations of your life. Just as surely as a criminal is in the penitentiary as the result of conduct through which he reflected a very negative personality, so is every reader of this book where he is, because of his personality as reflected through his conduct.

With these two important statements this chapter will be closed:

1. **A pleasing personality will help you to market your services effectively.**

2. **Sound character will help you to keep your services marketed permanently.**

CHAPTER 17
Cooperation

Cooperation is a quality without which no person can hope to market his personal services effectively! It is a quality which must become a habit with all who make themselves indispensable to their employers.

The late Andrew Carnegie said inability to cooperate stood at the head of the list of the causes of failure. Moreover, he emphasized the fact that lack of cooperation was one deficiency which he would not tolerate, no matter how well equipped in other ways a man might be. He amplified his statement by the explanation that a man who lacks the ability either to cooperate with others or to gain cooperation from others is a disturbing element whose influence spreads with disastrous results. He then stated his point conversely by saying that a man who not only cooperated with others, but who had the personality to induce others to cooperate with him, served as a powerful influence through which coordination of effort or teamwork could be produced.

He should know: he made cooperation pay.

Through a series of tests made by the late Dr. Alexander Graham Bell and others, it was discovered that one person of the fault-finding type in an organization of a thousand people would have the effect of coloring the mental attitude of everyone around him, thereby creating friction and dissatisfaction.

Success is achieved through power!

Power is developed through organized and intelligently directed knowledge. The intelligent use of knowledge calls for cooperation. Woe unto him who fails to understand and apply the principle of cooperative effort.

The time you put on a job is not the correct measure of your worth. That is determined by the quality and the quantity of your work, plus the influences you have on others by your mental attitude.

The larger corporations have already learned that cooperation among their employees is their greatest asset. It was the lack of this sort of cooperation that placed business at the mercy of labor racketeers.

It is only a question of time until every well managed business will have a system by which it may discover lack of cooperation among its employees. Friction among employees has been one of the greatest evils of the past in industry and business. The well-managed business of the future will insist upon an *esprit de corps* among its employees such as business management of the past has not demanded. Those who are capable of managing business successfully have learned that no business succeed without this spirit of *harmonious* cooperation. Moreover, the cooperative effort must be in spirit as well as in deed. This point is important so bear in mind.

I am stating these facts very plainly because I am convinced that no person can market himself effectively in the future without understanding and applying the principle of harmonious cooperation! Observe with profit the emphasis upon the word *harmony*. Cooperation, to be effective, must be more than tentative. It must be real and it must be based upon perfect harmony.

Indigestion, a bad liver, and auto-intoxication are a few of the causes of inability to cooperate. Grouchiness will turn out to be "ouchiness." This statement applies to the owner of the business a well as his employees. The public has learned to expect and demand efficient and pleasant service.

* * * * *

"Your position is nothing more than your opportunity to show what sort of ability you have. You will get out of it exactly what you put into it—no more and no less. A "big" position is but the sum total of numerous "little" positions well filled."

– Napoleon Hill

* * * * *

CHAPTER 18
How To Create A Job

Keen imagination is essential in all forms of salesmanship.

Imagination is of two forms. One is known as synthetic imagination and the other is known as creative imagination.

Synthetic imagination consists of combining or bringing together two or more known ideas, principles, concepts, or laws and giving them a new use. Practically all inventions are created through the faculty of synthetic imagination because they consist merely of a new combination of old principles and ideas, or of giving old ideas or principles a new use.

Creative imagination consists of interpretation of basically new ideas, plans, concepts, or principles which present themselves through the creative faculty and whose source is outside the range of the five senses of perception.

Imagination can be cultivated; it is a fascinating pursuit, rich with rewards.

We are concerned at this time mainly with the principle of synthetic imagination because this is the key-stone to the arch of selling either personal services or commodities of any description.

The faculty of imagination becomes more alert through use! In this respect it responds like any organ of the body or group of cells.

Some people have the mistaken notion that the imagination is complicated and that only geniuses make effective use of it.

Through the use of his imagination (while working as a telegraph operator), James J. Hill saw that the East should be connected with the West by a dependable railway system. His ability to see this was imagination which enabled him to build and operate the Great Northern Railway System. Any other man could have done it.

Organized imagination brings the highest price of any form of ability. It always has a market and it has no limitations as to value. "Business depressions" do not destroy the market for imagination; they merely increase the need and extend the demand for imagination. The world stands in need of men who will use their imaginations.

The most desirable and highest paid positions are those which men of imagination create for themselves. Business is stagnant all over the country. Use your imagination and discover ways and means of stimulating business, even in a very small way, in any line and you may name your own salary. The country is faced not by the necessity of solving one problem, but by the necessity of solving hundreds of problems. Pick out any one of these problems and work out, through your imagination, its solution and your problem of acquiring money will be solved.

> **Not all of the new ways of doing business nor the best ways have yet been found. The future will call for still more new ways. This need is your opportunity. Use your imagination and convert that opportunity into fortune.**

Take inventory of the shortcomings of the business in which you are employed and use your imagination for the purpose of eliminating some of them. Or if you are not employed, use your imagination to create some plan by which you may improve some part of any business with which you may be familiar and you will soon find a place for yourself. Positions can be made to order.

This is an age of rapid-fire change in business! It is an age which was made to order for men who have and use imagination. Because business is stagnant, business men will try almost anything. Create some new, unique idea that is sound and sell it to them!

If you are employed and find yourself worrying about the possibility of losing your job, convert the time you have been wasting on worry to a better use by creating some plan that will improve your work or add to your employer's business. You can make yourself indispensable in this way. Indispensability commands a high price and permanency of employment at all times.

* * * * *

"The greatest cure for loneliness, discouragement, and discontentment, is work that produces a healthy sweat!"

– Napoleon Hill

* * * * *

CHAPTER 19
How To Choose Your Occupation

Instructions have been offered for aiding those who wish to choose jobs intelligently. These instructions were not entirely adequate for the needs of young people who have just finished their schooling but have never held positions or chosen a vocation.

Decision in connection with the choice of a life work is one of the two most important decisions which young people have the responsibility of making. The other is the decision in connection with the selection of a mate in marriage.

These two decisions determine largely whether one's life shall be blessed with happiness and fortune or cursed with misery and poverty!

A decision as to a vocation suited to his or her needs is a very difficult matter for any inexperienced young person. Had I chosen my vocation at the end of my high school training I would have become a telegraph operator since this was the work that most appealed to my imagination at that time. Fortunately, a former school-mate who had been away attending business college came home for the Christmas holidays and, before returning, sold me on the idea of going with him. My decision to take a business training course proved to be one of the most important decisions of my life. In the first place, this training prepared me to earn a living. In the second place, it brought me into intimate contact with some of the greatest business and industrial leaders the country has ever known.

In the capacity of secretary, I literally went to school to the men for whom I worked and I am happy to acknowledge this part of my schooling was worth more than all the other schooling I received. I am convinced that every young man and women should take a business course and gain some experience at first hand in many lines of business before selecting a vocation. This gives one an opportunity to weigh and to consider the possibilities available in various fields of business and to make a choice of vocation that is based upon actual knowledge of the details of the chosen work.

Business training not only gave me the opportunity to go to school with some of the most able men in America, but that training proved to be a veritable source of insurance against catastrophe on more than a score of occasions during the twenty-five years of effort when I found it necessary to stop my research and earn money. There was never a time when I could not market the knowledge which I gained in business school for more than enough to take care of my living expenses.

Because of my business training, I was privileged to work for the late Dr. Elmer R. Gates and the late Dr. Alexander Graham Bell, inventor of the Long Distance Telephone. From both of them I received knowledge of a priceless nature. Through this training, too, I was privileged to work for a doctor from whom I received much of the biological data I needed, and for a noted lawyer from whom I gathered a knowledge of law and legal procedure which has been most helpful to me.

Training in business brought me the knowledge through which I obtained every promotion I ever had while working for a salary. To it I also owe the selection of my life's work, for it brought me into contact with Andrew Carnegie, Thomas A. Edison, Henry Ford, and most of the others who have been so helpful to me in the building of this philosophy.

Every young man and woman ought to be able to (1) operate a computer efficiently, (2) take notes speedily, and, (3) keep a set of books accurately, before selecting a vocation. Knowledge of these subjects is of vital importance in the successful conduct of any business or profession.

The modern business college is a sort of missing link between the public schools and the colleges and the field of business because the business college specializes in a form of training which is inadequately handled by the public schools. The public schools and colleges, although they should prepare young people for efficient service in business, do not. Moreover, I have learned from my experience in employing many young people, some of whom were graduates of commercial departments of high schools and others were graduates of modern business colleges, that the business college graduate is far superior to the graduate of the commercial departments of high schools.

A business college training is an absolute necessity to the person who aspires to a position as an executive in the field of business today for the reason that executives must have understudy experience of a nature which can be acquired only through business college preparation.

The modern business colleges of today have had the foresight to see the dawn of a new era of business ethics which has grown out of the depression and are preparing their graduates to adapt themselves to the new standards.

The public schools on the whole have not seen this need, or if they have seen it, they are doing nothing to equip students to meet it.

This chapter is intended solely for young people who have not yet selected a life work. If you are in that category, defer your decision as to a vocation until you have taken a complete business training and have applied that training for at least two years. Your decision then will be more sound than any you could make at this time, for it will provide an opportunity to go to school with successful men who will pay for the privilege of training you!

Business training, in my case, was the result of a chance or accidental decision. Your decision to market your services through the aid of a business college training should not be accidental; it should be by design.

There is no way of determining the actual value of the training I received in business college. First, because I am still in the prime of life and have before me what I consider the best part of my career, and second, because I have found through my business training the vocation which I like best and in which I am happy. Happiness and contentment cannot be measured in terms of bank balances alone. Were I forced to set a monetary value on my business college training, however, I would estimate it at no less than $1,000,000.00. Its total cost was approximately $500.00 in money and a year's time. The investment has yielded me more than adequate returns.

There is a certain atmosphere about a business college which is most helpful to young people because all of the students in attendance are thinking and talking in terms of rendering useful service. In the public schools and colleges of today, the atmosphere often takes on an entirely different tone which savors more of play than it does work.

The best results cannot be obtained in this way.

Mindful of the fact that some readers may wish to go from high school to college for the purpose of preparing themselves to take up a profession, I would particularly recommend that they take a business college training first. The competition in the professions today is very keen. Only those who understand the business foundation on which every profession must be conducted will survive. The large percentage of fatalities in the professions is due mainly to the fact that so many professional people know nothing about the fundamentals of business organization. Such knowledge is essential.

Moreover, the business college trained student can easily earn his way through college. I know many successful college graduates who paid their way through college. The person who can operate a computer efficiently and who can take notes rapidly, can get much more out of college than the person who lacks this skill.

Young woman usually begin to think in terms of marriage about the time they complete their high school training. While marriage is a lofty ambition, it brings responsibilities and creates emergencies which call for wise thought and action. The woman who has been schooled in a business college and who has had some experience in a business office is much better prepared to assume the practical responsibilities of a home than one who has had no such training. She not only is in position to cooperate with her husband in a spirit of sympathy and understanding in connection with his problems of earning a living, but if an occasion demands, the married woman who has had a business training may go back to it and earn a living. Business training, therefore, becomes a sort of insurance against dependence.

USE WISDOM IN YOUR SELECTION OF COLLEGE

No statement in this chapter should be interpreted as a blanket statement endorsement of all business colleges. Happily, most of the business colleges in the United States are efficient and their management consists of men and women who are conscientious. But, as in all other fields, there are some that are better equipped than others to render practical service. The first factor to be looked for in the selection of a business college is age. The college that has survived for a long number of years must have adequate equipment and competent teachers or it would not have lasted. The next factor to be considered is the business and ethical standing of the owner. The school whose practice or teaching is unethical cannot be long-lived. The third factor to be considered is the question of competency of its teachers.

A SUGGESTION FOR FINANCING YOURSELF THROUGH BUSINESS COLLEGE

Usually the young people who pay a portion or all of their expenses while taking a business or college training get more out of their training than those who do not pay any part of their expenses. I have delivered lectures to many groups of students. The students who work their way through college are the first to arrive and they occupy the front seats, while those whose expenses are paid by their parents usually arrive late and select seats well toward the rear of the auditorium where they can make a quick getaway as soon as the lectures are finished. Those who work take copious notes on the lectures, while those who do not work usually take no notes. I have no doubt that if I could follow these young men and women into the business world, I would find that the students who worked their way through college had much less difficulty in earning a living than those who did not.

I believe you'll agree with that statement.

The urge of necessity is a great blessing to most people. It forces them to do the things they should do, but too often

would not do, without the pressure of necessity. One reason business college graduates usually find less difficulty in marketing their services is the fact that most of them are attending business college because they come from families who know from experience the urge of necessity.

This is an age of unprecedented opportunity due mainly to the great need for leadership in practically every calling. Opportunity will be greatest for those who have had a thorough business training. This is an age which accepts young blood in positions of responsibility.

These greater opportunities of today call for greater efficiency than was acceptable twenty-five years ago. This machine age of efficiency in production has brought with it a demand for greater efficiency in manpower. The principles through which efficiency may be attained have been described in the pages of this book. Not one of these principles is difficult to develop or apply.

The principle to which I have reference is so simple that its importance may be underestimated by many, especially by the young person inexperienced in business.

The principle may be described as "The faith and persistence to accept defeat as being nothing more than an experience from which something of value is learned." Most people give up or let their ambition be killed when serious obstacles are met.

Life is filled with obstacles which must be surmounted. Only those who have the stamina and the willingness to fight can win. Others must take the count. Do not expect that you will be one of the "fortunate" who never meet with serious opposition in life, for you there will be no exception to the general rule. Everyone meets with opposition. Opposition should be accepted as a signal to put everything you have into its mastery.

It has been my privilege during my public career to know many men and women of great achievement. Some of them I have known intimately. All of them had met with opposition which necessitated struggle and persistence.

When defeat comes, as it will, accept it as a hurdle which has been placed in your way for the purpose of training you to jump higher! You will gain strength and skill from each hurdle that you surmount.

Do not hate people because they oppose you. Thank them for forcing you to develop the strategy and imagination you will need to master their opposition.

This is a beautiful world and life is stocked with an abundance of everything you need, including riches and happiness, which you may have, provided you do not over-indulge in the things you like best, nor permit yourself to be suppressed by the circumstance and things you do not like.

Accept both the bitter and the sweet of life's cup like a real sportsman, remembering the while that a well-rounded life requires some of each. Success without defeat would lead to autocracy and a consequent boredom. Defeat without the counteracting effect of success would kill ambition. Be willing to accept your portion of each, but do not expect success without temporary defeat, there is no such possibility.

Now, let us see what a popular writer says.

Ed Sullivan, the noted Hollywood newspaper columnist, wrote the climax of this chapter for you. His counsel may be of great value to any young person who thinks for a moment that one can crash the gates at Hollywood or any other place without paying the price of success.

"A few days ago, a Boston professor urged the graduating class to forget their ambitions—and go on relief. The class orator at New York University sounded the same refrain.

"Five hundred thousand graduated from American universities this month. Are the odds 500,000 to 1 against you? Certainly not. Fifty percent of that total will disqualify themselves by laziness, lack of ambition, refusal to accept responsibility, because I've found that half of the world is as intent on not succeeding as the other half is intent on success. So your opposition is sliced in half. Sickness, temperament, liquor, gambling will cut heavily into the remainder.

"The best dramatization of what I'm telling you is the Kentucky Derby. Last year, 110 horses were nominated for the derby. These nominees were well trained and coddled in every possible way that great trainers could devise. Of the 110 horses, only 10 of them went to the post. It's the same in everyday life. The odds are always less when the chips are on the lines.

"So don't worry about the opposition and competition that will be offered you. It will be much less than you expect. And don't worry, either, if you won't be able to go to college, now that you have finished high school. University of Southern California recently conferred a degree of master of science on a boy who never even finished high school, Walt Disney.

"It wasn't so long ago that Disney and his brother, Roy, didn't have enough money to eat decently. They'd go into a restaurant and order one dinner, with two sets of knives, forks, and spoons.

"You'd think, from the present goings-on, that these days are so extraordinary that the present generation should have medals struck off in their honor. It's not so. The successful men and women of this motion picture industry all had to work their way up from poor homes. Times always have been tough for the poor.

"Paul Muni was a poor boy. Sam Goldwyn was a glove salesman. David O. Selznick is the son of a rich man who went broke. Louis B. Mayer, the power at MGM, recalls when his family didn't have enough to eat. Disney was ridiculed, and shoved around by shrewder business men.

"Had any of them been quitters, you would not know of them today. They had ambition and courage. They were tenacious. Nobody shoved them upstairs. Nobody created jobs for them, or told them how to hang on once the job was secured. Just as nobody can tell you what to do, or how to get it. You've got to learn that yourself; you've got to adapt yourself to conditions, and that is a personal issue.

"If you listened to the radio in recent years you heard the broadcast of two fights, the Joe Louis-Max Baer fight, and the Henry Armstrong-Barney Ross fight. Baer quit, and you heard the referee count him out while Baer rested on one knee. In the Armstrong-Ross fight, Ross took a terrible lacing, but refused to let his handlers or the referee stop the fight.

"In life, you can take the count on one knee, as Max Baer did, or you can imitate Barney Ross. You can quit or you can carry on. I'll let you decide which to emulate.

"You are living in an age that is distinguished for the greatest liberalism that ever has been focused on the American scene. Legislators are occupying themselves with the problems of the poor, which didn't happen years ago. There are CCC camps and the WPA; the world is interested in relieving distress in much greater measure than ever before. Governments actually tell off dictators and speak in behalf of weaker nations. All of these things are encouraging.

"So, to all of you kids who are starting out, don't be too overwhelmed by surface indications. The weather forecast still is weather clear, track fast, and rewards are greater than ever before. Don't ask too much of life, that's all. In the final analysis, if you get just a little success, and a lot of love, they'll hold up your hand as the winner."

*   *   *   *   *

"The happiest people are those who have learned to mix play with their work and to bind the two together with enthusiasm!"

– Napoleon Hill

*   *   *   *   *

CHAPTER 20
How To Budget Your Time

Before you can market your personal services effectively, you must lay out a program for yourself based upon an appropriate budget of your time. Nothing will be of greater assistance than compliance with this suggestion, a fact which will be surprising when you begin to make up your first time budget; surprising because of your discovery of the amount of time you have been wasting through lack of a budget. All well-managed businesses are operated on a budget system. The marketing of your services is a business. Moreover, to you it is the most important business in the world. It is a business which you can conduct efficiently only by organizing the hours at your disposal so they will yield a greater return than you could get from them without a budget.

Experience has proved that the following schedule is one which the majority of people can easily follow. It has also proved that it is an efficient schedule.

8 hours for sleep

8 hours for one's vocation

4 hours for recreation and health

2 hours for study and preparation

**2 hours for extra service for the benefit
   of others, without pay**

———

24 hours

Take inventory of yourself before creating any plans for marketing your personal services effectively and budget your time as nearly as possible to conform to this schedule.

Your attention is called emphatically to the last two periods of two hours each. These are the most profitable hours because the use which you make of these hours will determine more than any other factor whether or nor you market your services effectively.

You will observe that this schedule calls for two hours a day which must be devoted to study and preparation for greater efficiency in connection with your occupation. The majority of people have no such provision in their time budget—if, in fact, they have any budget.

You will also observe that the schedule includes two definite hours which must be devoted to rendering extra service for which one is not paid. This fixes approximately the time which one must put into one's work in following the habit of rendering service which is greater in quantity than one is paid for. The proportion is one-fourth of the time allotted for one's vocation. If you follow this schedule you will find ways and means of doing approximately one-fourth more work in the future than you have been doing in the past. The majority of people can easily follow this part of the schedule. It does not mean that one must be on duty 12 hours a day instead of 8. It means that one should accomplish in eight hours as much as one has heretofore been accomplishing in twelve hours.

These additional two hours of quantity of service may be rendered in many ways other than by merely being on the job two hours longer. For example, the equivalent of two extra hours may be delivered by:

1. *Greater cooperation with fellow employees and management*
2. *Personal conduct which constitutes a more pleasing personality*
3. *Greater skill in connection with one's efforts*
4. *Working with a definite goal or amount of work to be performed as salesmen work on definite sales quotas*

5. *Working in a spirit of enthusiasm and genuine interest.*

The following schedule represents fairly the budget actually followed by the average person because of indifference:

THE TIME BUDGET ONE SHOULD NOT FOLLOW

8 hours for labor which is performed with one eye on the time clock and one's thoughts on quitting time

8 hours of sleep

8 hours for miscellaneous dissipation of one's energies ranging all the way from parties and habits of intemperance in eating, drinking, and sex indulgences to even more destructive habits

------

24 hours

Check this schedule carefully and compare it with your use of time. This will constitute a most important part of your self-analysis. Check yourself against this schedule with courage and frankness. Do not make the mistake of giving yourself the benefit of all doubts. Reverse the rule and analyze yourself with merciless accuracy. Remember again that you are where you are and what you are because of your own conduct. Find out if your conduct is lifting you up the ladder of success or lowering you to failure.

By the time you are through with this self-analysis you may catch a glimpse of some of the habits which have been standing between you and the station in life you would like to attain. Also, you may reach the conclusion that there is something which you must do for yourself in marketing your personal services effectively. Unless you are an unusual person this analysis will bring to your attention many changes of habits which you must make before you can hope to market your personal services effectively.

You cannot be successful without paying the price of success!

The price which must be paid has been clearly described. Not the least important of this price is definitely outlined in this chapter.

Before any reputable physician will undertake to prescribe a remedy for the ills of a patient, he will insist upon making a thorough diagnosis to ascertain what are the patient's ills. Diagnosis is the most important part of the physician's work. The same is true of the person who markets personal services effectively. He must begin by ascertaining what are his weaknesses and when they have been discovered, he must form habits which will either eliminate or bridge those weaknesses so they will not work against him.

This book will probably be of little value to all who through either neglect or indifference fail to follow the plan of self-analysis here described.

Before leaving this chapter I feel impelled to ask the reader to analyze the last 8 hour period of the time budget one should not follow. I have helped a large number of men and women to emancipate themselves from misery and want by aiding them in making an analysis of this eight hour period of the day which constitutes the pivotal point in one's life, at which failure may be turned into success or success into failure as the result of the way these eight hours are used.

Let it be clearly understood that I am not a reformer, nor have I any bill of complaint against those who wish to relax through play which may not be entirely conventional, because play and relaxation are just as important as labor and study. That which I have to say to the readers of this book in the subsequent paragraphs of this chapter is intended as a warning to those who devote the entire eight hour period to what they call relaxation and play.

This is a divas and sex age which has been keyed up to the highest pitch of action. If it is stepped up to much higher, the insane asylums will be filled with those who have cracked up. Millions of people who ought to be seriously interested in marketing their services effectively have been caught in this maelstrom of speed which is whirling them around ever faster and faster until they have completely lost balance.

These pleasure bound unfortunates not only use up to eight hours in the mad whirl, but they cut in on the eight hour period allotted for sleep and use up from two to six hours of that period. This has the effect of cutting into the eight hour period allotted for work and robbing it of two to six hours through lowered efficiency!

I know a great number of young people still in their twenties who look old and have far too little endurance. These young people are shortening their own lives and robbing themselves of the most vital asset they possess in marketing their services effectively.

This human body is so organized that it requires eight hours of complete relaxation in sleep out of every twenty-four. Human society is so organized that at least eight hours out of every twenty-four must be devoted to rendering useful service in one form or another. These two eight-hour periods cannot be whittled down or robbed for other purposes without a price, which means failure. The third period of eight hours is the only period that one can afford to gamble with under any circumstances!

This third eight-hour period holds the key to one's future. We are all more or less the victims of habit.

The two eight-hour periods allotted to work and sleep by their very nature more or less force one to acquire sane habits. If a person chooses to steal time from the eight-hour sleep period, nature steps in sooner or later and stops the practice temporarily by sending him to the hospital. If a person misappropriates a part of the eight-hour work period, the law of economic necessity steps in and calls a halt, a one must have food and clothing and a place to sleep.

The third eight-hour period, however, is a freelance period which may be either wasted in dissipation or used as a period of preparation for greater efficiency and greater earning capacity, as one elects.

Watch your habits during this eight-hour period because those habits hold the secret of your future, no matter who you are or what may be your calling in life. This period offers the only hope available to the person who is poverty stricken but desires riches. It is the starting point of the person who aspires to a position of independence and freedom.

When you come to analyze yourself for the purpose of discovering how many of the causes of failure are standing in your way, you will discover that most, if not all, of those disclosed by your analysis have grown out of your habits of waste during this eight-hour period.

If you work for others and desire promotion and larger income, you will find the answer in this eight-hour recreational period. You will find it nowhere else!

We are all victims of the power of suggestion. Most of out habits are acquired through the influence of other people around us. This is an age of wasteful, destructive habits and the price of escape from these habits is eternal vigilance. It is a price which must be paid by every person who markets his personal services effectively.

Drinking parties are very exciting. To some they are very interesting. To all they are destructive! If you have not the will power to resist the temptation to join your friends in parties of this kind, you had better look for new friends whose habits will tempt you in a more profitable direction. These parties, so popular in this age, collect a heavy toll in two ways from all who indulge in them: their victims pay in loss of efficiency which means loss of earning capacity, and they pay sooner or later in loss of health.

Young people can, because of the endurance of youth, make tremendous inroads upon their vitality without apparent effects. There comes a time, however, when these debts against one's health must be paid. Nature attends to this! She keeps a set of books in which every item is recorded. Moreover, she forces the individual to become his or her own bookkeeper. The charges compiled through the indiscretions of youth are collected through the infirmities of old age. A little while ago, I was called to a hospital to visit a former schoolmate whose habits of youth have piled up a huge account against his old age reserve. He had not yet reached old age, but his account had been so grossly overdrawn that nature brought him into the debtor's court for settlement. He was suffering from partial paralysis of the brain! In plain English, he was on the road to insanity.

All this may sound like a prohibitionist's preachment against drink. It is more than that. This acquaintance had cut himself down through excesses in eating, drinking, and sexual expression for over ten years, using up his eight-hour recreational period and making serious inroads upon the other two. I went to see him at the hospital for the purpose of helping him out of his financial difficulties. Excesses take a financial toll as well as a physical toll.

I have never desired to be a reformer or a preacher! This is a book on the subject of marketing personal services effectively. Nothing can be marketed *effectively* unless the product to be marketed has value. It has been my aim throughout these pages to describe what constitutes valuable services. It is hoped that some suggestion or statement may throw light upon your own situation and point out the way to a more effective marketing of your personal services.

During my public career I have observed the methods used by thousands of successful men in selling their way through life. Space does not permit a description of the methods used by all of these men, but I have chosen from the group one man whose principles of selling himself are described in detail.

The man chosen is Henry Ford, known the world over for his ability to get whatever he wants without violating the rights of his fellowman. I have chosen Ford for my analysis of men who successfully sell their way through life because he has used the self-same principles every successful person must use.

I have chosen Ford for the reason that I have had the privilege of closely observing him over so long a period of years that I feel sure I understand the principles underlying his success.

Do not browse through the Ford analysis or read it hurriedly. It is worthy of slow reading and careful analysis because it conveys the material of which you may easily build your own successful life. The story has not been included to glorify Ford. The sole purpose in publishing it is to place in the hands of every reader an accurate outline of the plans and principles which have made America's most successful businessman the success that everyone knows him to be.

You are especially requested to study carefully the rating given Ford on the *Principles of Individual Achievement*. After you finish reading this book come back to the Ford analysis and take inventory of yourself, measuring yourself honestly and frankly by these principles. If you do this faithfully you may discover what are the major points of difference between you and Henry Ford. The discovery, if accurately made, may both shock and benefit you!

It is well worth trying.

This book on personal promotion would hardly be complete without a description of the methods by which the world's leading industrialist lifted himself from poverty to plenty. As you read the analysis of Henry Ford's astounding achievements you should remember he was no outstanding genius at the start, had but little schooling, and was a pioneer in a new industry at a time when the entire country was unfriendly toward him and his "horseless buggy."

Do not make the mistake of assuming that Ford began in an age blessed with greater opportunities than those available at the present. The truth is just the opposite, and coincidental as it may seem, Ford's influence on civilization has actually had much to do with creating the more extensive opportunities which exist today. His influence has helped to bring the country and the city dweller into closer contact because of the wonderful system of good roads that belts the entire nation. He has provided employment for more people than any other man living. He has proved that an American citizen may start at scratch, without pull or financial backing, and accumulate a vast fortune without violating the rights of others. I wish to emphasize one truth above all others, namely, the principles employed by Ford in his climb to opulence are understandable and usable by any person who has the ambition to appropriate them.

Did you ever think of that?

Ford is a self-made man in the true sense of the term. If ever a man sold his way through life successfully, with his own brain and his own ideas, that man is Henry Ford. His story has been included in this book because his entire life represents one of the finest jobs of selling the world has ever known. There has been no scandal connected with the Ford methods of selling. He has helped everyone whom he has influenced. Every dollar of his fortune is being used constructively. He has established an all-time high standard of business ethics, which every other individual might do well to emulate.

I have begun my analysis of Ford by describing the one principle which, more than all others, has been responsible for the stupendous success he has achieved, the principle of singleness of purpose. That was all Ford had as an operating capital to begin with, but it was enough. Remember this, you who wish to emulate Ford, and remember too, that you are reading an analysis of the number one citizen and successful business man of the entire world.

* * * * *

"You have the power to create anything you can imagine! With proper action on the ideas produced by your imagination, you will achieve success!"

– **Napoleon Hill**

* * * * *

CHAPTER 21

Your Masterplan
For Getting A Position

T here is a definite, sure-fire method by which anyone may procure any position for which he is qualified. I will describe the method in detail, but first take notice I did not say that this plan would enable anyone to hold any job he might procure. Getting a job is one thing; holding it is something else. In as much as the major portion of this book has been devoted to a description of the principles by which people hold jobs I will not here repeat what I have stated on that subject.

I have been asked often, "How did you manage to interview all those successful men who helped you to organize the Law of Success philosophy? How did you induce them to give up so much of their time?" My answer is, "It is simple to get the opportunity to talk with men if you approach them through some subject in which they are interested, and do most of your talking about them!"

I might say the same thing in connection with procuring a position. It is easy to get any position one wants, providing one has the ability to fill it and makes the right sort of approach in applying for the position.

Through the pages, which follow, I am addressing men and women who are interested in procuring some sort of a position, or some form of personal contact requiring the cooperation of one or more people. The advice I offer is intended solely for the general guidance of anyone seeking to get the cooperation of others. The details should be changed to fit the particular needs of each individual, and should not be copied verbatim form this book. Your own judgement will tell you what to do,.

Let us assume you are desirous of procuring a position with the Standard Oil Company; that you are willing to start anywhere the company wishes to place you, your major desire being an opportunity to demonstrate what sort of services you can render.

Very well, here is a step by step outline of the approach which, if changed to fit your particular personality, could hardly fail to get you your desired opportunity.

FIRST: Decide what particular position with the Standard Oil Company you desire, then make a complete list, in writing, of all your qualifications to fill that position. If you feel the list of your capabilities is inadequate, after you have placed it on paper, go to work and prepare yourself through study and observation of some other person who is filling a position similar to the one you want, until you are sure you are ready for the position.

SECOND: Write out a list of the following seventeen principles of success and grade yourself accurately on each, the grade running from zero to 100% on each principle. Under each of the principles state in detail why you believe you are entitled to the credit you have given yourself, what definite proof you have to offer that your grading is accurate.

A DEFINITE MAJOR AIM IN LIFE ...._____%

Under this heading describe your major purpose in life, show that it is connected with the position you are seeking with the Standard Oil Company. If the particular position you wish is only to serve as a stepping stone, and you are aiming for a higher place, say so and give your reasons for believing you can advance to the better position.

SELF CONFIDENCE.................................._____%

State your reason for the grading you give yourself on this principle, and clearly indicate that you know the difference between self-confidence and egotism.

INITIATIVE..._____%

Under this heading give illustrations of occasions on which you have acted without supervision, on your own initiative, and state to what extent this procedure is a habit with you.

THE HABIT OF SAVING........................._____%

Under this heading make it clear that you have formed the habit of budgeting both your time and your income, and that you recognize the necessity of this sort of self-discipline as a means of attaining the object of your Major Aim in life.

IMAGINATION ...._____%

Give illustrations of occasions on which you have used your imagination. The best possible method by which you can do this impressively will be to indicate to what extent you used imagination in familiarizing yourself with the requirements of the position you are seeking.

ENTHUSIASM ...._____%

State to what extent you have your enthusiasm under control, and indicate your knowledge of the difference between passive and active enthusiasm. Indicate that your greatest enthusiasm is associated with your desire to procure and fill the position you are seeking with the Standard Oil Company, giving your reasons for your enthusiasm.

SELF CONTROL......................................._____%

Give your reasons for your grading on this principle, and state definitely how you make application of the principle as a means of striking a balance between your head and your heart, or in other words state to what extent you use self-discipline to help your head manage your emotions. Above all else, indicate that your self-control is sufficient to enable you to avoid becoming involved in controversies of other people; that it is sufficient to enable you to *think* for yourself, without the aid of elf-appointed leaders or propagandists.

THE HABIT OF DOING MORE THAN YOU ARE PAID TO DO ...._____%

Here is your big opportunity to land the position you are seeking. Give a detailed statement of why you have formed the habit of doing more work and better work than you are paid to do. This is the most important of the seventeen principles, as far as the procuring of a position is concerned. Moreover, it is the principle of major importance in connection with the holding of a position after you procure it, therefore make a strong statement a to your reasons for observing this principle as a part of your philosophy of life.

A PLEASING PERSONALITY ...._____%

In explaining your reasons for your rating on this important principle, give at least five definite illustrations of qualities you have which entitle you to rate as having a pleasing personality. Above all, give a detailed statement of your personal attitude toward others, whether it is at all times friendly and cooperative, and describe your disposition in negotiating with friends, relatives and business associates.

Life's battles don't always go to the stronger or faster man. But sooner or later the man who wins is the man who thinks he can.

ACCURATE THINKING ...._____%

Make it clear that you are grading yourself, on this important principle, only as it applies to your relationship to the position you are seeking. Give your reasons for believing you can think accurately in connection with the position you are seeking, and be sure they are based upon facts easily discernable from your statements.

CONCENTRATION OF EFFORT....................._____%

State clearly your reasons for your grading on your ability to concentrate your mind upon a any given task and keep it there until that task has been completed. Be sure, also, to indicate the extent to which you have formed the habit of concentrating your willpower upon the attainment of your Major Aim in life.

COOPERATION ...._____%

Clearly describe your reasons for following the habit of working with other people in a spirit of harmony, and explain that you do this not merely on occasion, but as a matter of continuous habit.

PROFITING BY FAILURES ...._____%

No one is expected to be infallible, therefore state frankly that you make mistakes but indicate to what extent you try to avoid duplicating, and be sure to describe how you manage to profit by your own failures and failures of other people. Indicate, also, that you know the difference between failure and temporary defeat, and say that you never accept defeat as anything more than an inspiration to make a fresh and more determined start.

TOLERANCE ...._____%

In explaining your grading on this important subject clearly indicate that you understand tolerance to mean "An open mind on all subjects, toward all people." Be sure to describe the extent to which you practice tolerance.

THE GOLDEN RULE APPLIED ...._____%

Grade yourself on your application of this great law of human conduct, and explain why you follow the habit of placing yourself in the other fellow's place when reaching decisions which in any way affect him.

THE HABIT OF HEALTH ...._____%

In explaining your grading on this subject, be sure to indicate that you do not suffer with imaginary symptoms of illness, that you follow the habit of attending to your diet, exercise and elimination, and be sure to indicate clearly that you do not have a bad disposition due to your failure to keep your sewer system cleaned out.

THE MASTER MIND APPLIED ...._____%

The "Master Mind" is principle through which one or more people may coordinate their efforts in a spirit of perfect harmony, for a definite purpose. Indicate definitely that you understand the value of such coordination of effort, that you follow the habit of observing this important principle, and explain how you believe you can make use of it in connection with the position you are seeking.

After you have graded yourself on the foregoing seventeen principles of personal achievement, write the following letter, or some modified form of it, and mail the letter to letter to the manager of the department of the Standard Oil Company in which you are seeking a position:

Mr. Walter Teagle, President,
Standard Oil Company
New York City

My dear Mr. Teagle:

With this letter I am sending you an accurate statement of the reasons why I deserve the position of _____ with your company. With this statement I am sending also, an accurate grading of myself on each of the seventeen principles of success, together with a detailed explanation under each principle as to why the grade was given.

Now here is the condition under which I ask you to give me the position I am seeking:

Let me work in the position for one month, without compensation. At the end of the month if I have not demonstrated, beyond all question of doubt, that I have the sort of material in me that any great corporation such as the Standard Oil Company would naturally be seeking, I will step aside. Additionally, before doing so, I will pay your company a reasonable sum to reimburse it for the actual cost of the supervision given to me during the month's trial. (omit this last offer, if you choose)

If you want the trial period to go beyond one month that will be satisfactory with me. All I ask, during the demonstration, is that you allow me to put into my work the hours and the sort of effort I believe to be necessary to prove that I am not merely just another person seeking a job. What I am really seeking is not a job, but an opportunity to earn a place as _____ in your company.

Will you give me this opportunity?

Very Cordially,

_____

Have the letter neatly typed, and also have your grading on the seventeen principles of achievement, and your statement of reasons why you believe yourself qualified for the position you seek, typed.

If you desire to apply for a position with several different firms, send a similar letter, with the grading and the statement of your capabilities, to each firm. However, be sure to take the time to investigate each different firm's methods of doing business, its problems, etc., so you will be in a position to make your application fit the job you seek.

In grading yourself on the seventeen principles use your own imagination and so word your explanations of your gradings that the person to whom you are applying for a position will quickly see that you are familiar with the requirements of such a position.

Remember, as you prepare your application for a position, that you will be practically sure to get a favorable hearing if you so word your letter and your grading that you definitely convey the impression you are willing to prove your ability before asking anyone to purchase your services.

Remember, also, that you will not receive encouragement unless you choose some position in which a person of your personality, education, race and experience is needed. Do sufficient advance investigation to convince yourself the position for which you apply really needs you, then go after it and sell yourself to the man who has the yes or the no over the job.

Do not make the mistake of grading yourself too high on all the seventeen principles. Grade yourself down on at least a few of them, and explain why your rating is not higher. I once knew a young man to apply for a position through this plan who was so lacking in modesty that he graded himself 100% on each of the seventeen principles. It might have helped him had he known that not even Henry Ford could accurately grade himself that high.

If you do a good job of grading yourself, and go into details to show how you arrived at your rating, you will have a marvelous sales letter that will interest the right person in your services, in the grading alone. Remember, as you explain each of the gradings, that your explanation is in fact your strongest selling argument in your behalf.

The day that you mail your application send the following telegram to the person to whom you send the application, and do not forget to prepay the message:

It is well worth remembering that the client or customer is the most important factor in any business. If you don't think so, try to get along without him or her for awhile.

Walter Teagle, President
Standard Oil Company
New York City

In today's mail I am sending you an important letter which I hope your
secretary will deliver to you promptly.

_____

Attach a good unmounted photograph of yourself to your letter; one
that has been recently taken.

Send with the letter the names and addresses of five references,
preferably people engaged in established businesses, or bankers.

State your age, nationality, and schooling.

If your application is properly prepared, and you select with care the
firms to whom you send it, you can safely count on procuring a position
if you include at least ten different firms on your list. In other words you
will be practically sure of finding what you want be seeking for it in ten
different directions.

*Let me emphasize that you should use your own imagina-
tion and initiative when it comes to the actual writing of the
letter of application.* The only thing you should not change is the
policy of offering your services for one month, or longer, strictly on trial.
Everything else in the letter may be altered to suit your personality, or to
make the letter fit your needs to better advantage.

If you follow these instructions carefully and fail to get the results you
desire, you may send the author a copy of your letter and your personal
grading on the seventeen principles of success and he will determine
wherein you have failed. Be prepared, however, to back up all you
promise in your letter, in the event that you are given a trial. Any lack of
sincerity on your part will be quickly detected, if you are given a position,
and this will not help your case.

I may as well tell you here and now that there always has been a place,
and there always will be a place, for a man or a woman who has ability
and sincerely follows the habit of rendering more service and better

service than that for which he or she is paid. No matter how many business depressions may come and go, there will always be a place for the person willing to render such service. Moreover, the rendering of service in this spirit is the surest way to promotion.

If you grade yourself accurately on each of the seventeen principles of success, and discover after completing your grading that your percentage is too low on any of the principles, you will have made a valuable discovery about yourself. This discovery, if acted upon, will enable you to prepare yourself to bridge whatever weakness you may possess. This grading should prove to be a profitable check-up on yourself, and it might well turn out to be the most important turning-point of your life, providing it brings you face to face with yourself and portrays your personality as it really exists.

You need this self-analysis, whether you wish to use it to procure a position or not. Everyone needs such a check-up, and especially during these times, when so many people are trying to get something for nothing, and thousands are killing off their initiative, self-confidence and definiteness of purpose to go on Government Relief. If you are willing to throw yourself on charity and live without rendering useful service, this analysis will do you no good. It is intended only for the person who wishes to be self-determining and who truly is willing to earn whatever he demands in life.

After preparing the copy for your letter of application, and your personal grading on the seventeen principles, if you have a feeling that your case has not been properly prepared you may send a copy of your letter and grading to the author. Either, he or one of his assistants, will look over your work and offer such suggestions for its improvement as may seem to be needed. Under no circumstances, however, will the author or his assistants undertake to write the copy for these documents.

You now have in your hands, in this simple plan, the finest of all possible methods of selling yourself into any position for which you are qualified. The psychology back of the plan has been tried in thousands of cases, and I have never known it to fail to produce the desired results. The spirit of the plan is far more important than the mere wording of the application. Let me emphasize the importance of truth: It is so seldom that any person applies for a position on this sort of basis, that those who do so benefit by the law of contrast. Not one executive out of a hundred would refuse to investigate the merits of a person offering to work on the basis of demonstrating his ability before trying to collect pay. You know that some of the largest corporations in the world have regular employee "talent scouts" out searching for young men and young women with just such a spirit of willingness to render service as the one here described? When such a person is found he or she is quickly employed, and the gates to quick advancement are eternally left ajar.

One Final Word: If you find the seventeen principles helpful in procuring an opportunity to demonstrate your ability, think how much more helpful they may be if you make intelligent application of these principles after you get your foot in the door! In other words, do not stop by using these universal principles of success to induce someone to give you a position, but go further and so use these principles that you can collect whatever you want or demand of life.

*   *   *   *   *

"There are no lazy men. What may appear to be a lazy man is only an unfortunate person who has not found the work for which he is best suited."

– Napoleon Hill

*   *   *   *   *